REAL WOMEN
LOVE FOOTY

REAL WOMEN LOVE FOOTY

Dawn Leicester & Penny Mackieson

Lothian BOOKS

For our dads, Glyn and Lionel,
for sharing with us the love of the game.

Thomas C. Lothian Pty Ltd
132 Albert Road, South Melbourne 3205
www.lothian.com.au

National Library of Australia
Cataloguing-in-Publication data:

Leicester, Dawn.
Real women love footy.

ISBN 0 7344 0603 7.

1. Australian football - Anecdotes. 2. Football fans -
Australia - Anecdotes. I Mackieson, Penny. II. Title.
796.336

Cover design by Andrew Cunningham
Internal design by Paulene Meyer
Cover photography by Ian Kenins
Printed in Australia by Griffin Press

Foreword

From the moment I came to live in Melbourne in the mid-eighties, I realised there was something different about this town.

It happened around the office water-coolers on Monday mornings and built to a crescendo by weekend as the tribes readied for battle once again.

Luckily, as a young ABC reporter, I soon got a taste for what all the fuss was about.

I was sent off as one of the first women ever to report on the then VFL tribunal. Those were the days when the truth was never told, and minding their language because a woman was in the room was the least of the players' worries.

As the year played out there were the endless machinations of week by week match-ups, as injury brought dreams to an end and fairytale stories played out as new football stars were born.

Then there was the build-up to grand final week, the Brownlow, the parade, as the combatants readied for a winner-takes-all one day in September.

Not surprisingly, by the end of my first year I was hooked,

I had chosen my team — the Demons — and I happily allowed the great tribal traditions of Aussie Rules footy to envelop me.

And it is in this spirit that Penny and Dawn have lovingly crafted their passion in the stories in this book. There are the generational rites of passage, the tricky allegiances that come with choosing your favourite player and the champagne world of female football fans.

For those of us who love it know it is much more than a sport; it's embedded deep in our culture, the rivalries are about so much more than the clashes on the football field … but it's a passion none of us would be without.

Their stories give you a glimpse of what some of you might be missing out on!

BEV O'CONNOR

Bev is Vice-President of the Melbourne Football Club, as well as an ABC sports presenter.

Contents

Acknowledgements

This is not only our first book together but our very first book, and it's been an incredible adventure.

Thank you to Bev O'Connor for lending valuable support to our project and capturing in one page what we've attempted to do in 220.

Thank you to our parents — Glyn and Dorothy, and Lionel and Lois — for a lifetime of love and encouragement. We couldn't have achieved this without the love and support of our boys — Hugh, Bruce and Patrick — we sincerely hope you think all the pain was worth it.

To the Collingwood and Melbourne Football Clubs, thank you for the proud history and real passion that is such an important part of our lives.

Finally, thank you to all of the passionate women football supporters who understand that footy is much more than a man's game and are such an inspiration to us.

About the Authors

Dawn Leicester and **Penny Mackieson** live and breathe football. After meeting in 1980 while studying at Melbourne University then sharing a flat together, Dawn and Penny's football-friendship has culminated in writing this book about their experiences. They're Real Women and they just Love their Footy!

Penny and Dawn at Copeland Trophy Night 2001.

Dawn was born in England and emigrated to Australia in 1971. She inherited her father's love of sport and has been a passionate Collingwood fan since arriving in Melbourne in 1972. Dawn is a proud Collingwood member and a member of the Women in Black coterie. Outside of football, she pursues a career in banking and is married to Hugh Leicester.

Penny grew up in rural eastern Victoria. A Melbourne Demons fan all her life, she hero-worshipped Robbie Flower as a teenager and is a devoted member of the Melbourne Football Club and its She Devils coterie. Penny is a Social Worker in the field of children's and family services. She is married to Bruce Minahan, a Collingwood fan, and they have a son, Patrick — another keen Demons supporter!

Introduction
Around the Grounds and Back Again

Whose bright idea was it to write this book? You may well ask. To be completely honest, it's a bit hard to say — it seems to have happened so long ago that it's difficult to untangle. We have been friends since meeting at university in 1980. Dawn always wanted to be a writer — it was a question of *when would she get around to it*? And Penny has produced several professional works. So the idea of writing a book didn't seem too outlandish. The real surprise to our friends and family was probably more that the subject of our collective work is football.

It's probably also a surprise to some that our partnership has been so successful, given our totally different styles. We don't mind admitting that on paper we appear to be a creative partnership designed for tears. Penny describes herself as a well-organised (some may even say, 'anally retentive') person who prepares, makes notes, researches, drafts, improves and polishes her work well before deadlines. In contrast, Dawn is a classic last-minute operator who has done much of her best work in the last hours before a paper was due. It can be frustrating waiting for something from Dawn because she creates the piece in her head and can only produce it when the moment is right. Of course, when it does pour out, it's much like a monsoonally flooded river of consciousness!

The funny thing is that, while we each knew that the other loved football and the respective teams we followed, we didn't spend much time talking about the great game when we were studying together. Nowadays, we can't imagine why we didn't. But that's how it was. And certainly neither of us attended many AFL matches, or VFL as it was then. The germination of this book may possibly have occurred a few years later, in 1983–4, when we shared a flat together.

> We have very fond memories from that
> time; of sessions together with wine casks
> and Twisties, viewing telecasts of the
> Brownlow Medal count on TV.

But getting back to the question of who is responsible for the idea of writing this book … Penny insists on shouldering at least some of the burden of responsibility. In 1998 she presented Dawn with a rather unusual gift on her birthday. The gift comprised several typed pages inserted into a plastic folder bearing the title page, 'A Woman's Guide to Enjoying Football or, alternatively, A Woman's Guide to the Ultimate Football Experience by Dawn Carringbush and Penny de Ville'. The folder formed part of a challenge to Dawn to co-write with Penny a book that would be a practical guide to being a female Aussie Rules supporter.

Dawn was more than a bit keen on the idea and the process kicked off. After a flurried start, we quickly proceeded to tighten the concept for our book and commenced the research phase. The 'research' was, of course, most essential. It required getting involved in relevant coteries within our respective clubs, attending as many club functions as we could afford, and conducting interviews with relevant club officials and female supporters. All this was, of course, additional to our regular attendance at matches. We really enjoyed our research (so much so that it continues to this day!), although some of our friends struggled to understand what it had to do with football. We particularly enjoyed the dinner dances and lunches, which many of our 'struggling' friends also enjoyed — we don't know any women who dislike dressing up for a party! We even travelled interstate with a friend to watch Collingwood play the Crows … a story in itself!

While throwing ourselves into the research, we simultaneously started generating alternative ideas about the approach our book should take and suitable titles to match. Initially, we were both very keen on the 'how to enjoy football' idea. This idea started to fade, however, when we discovered a book written by a female sports reporter that provided a guide for women to the four major football codes played in Australia.

The 'how to enjoy football' idea was finally extinguished after we attended a women's coterie function in 2000 — the Grand Final Week Breakfast for the Collingwood Football Club. The guest speaker discussed the book she had just written about how to be a good football fan. The concept of the book — to provide some advice, based on her own experiences, to football fans with a view to helping them maximise their enjoyment of the game — was very, *very* similar to our original idea. It was obviously time to rethink.

Luckily we weren't precious ... actually, we had already moved on! We decided to expand on the idea of interviewing female supporters and to write the book as a series of chapters, each one consisting of an interview with a female supporter, some well-known to the public, others we had met through our own football-going and research. The interviews were to cover how each woman became interested and involved in football and in her chosen club; any notable football experiences she'd had — good, bad, funny, etcetera; her reflections on how she most enjoys the game; and possibly also her advice for other female supporters. The idea was to share the stories of women who are passionate about football.

Dawn wanted to be very thorough and was keen to interview women involved in each of the sixteen AFL clubs, or at least from a selection of the clubs in each state. Penny wasn't so keen on that part of the idea; she felt a major historic work or, at the very least, a Masters thesis coming on, not to mention a Visa account that would take three years to pay off!

However, this idea did evolve and gather momentum. We even prepared a serious book proposal that included a substantial list of potential interviewees. It lasted right up until one day when Penny was in a bookshop perusing the sports section, as you do, and she noticed a book compiled by a highly successful AFL coach and a female sports writer. Their book was based on interviews with women who are all either well known in their own right or associated with well-known football personalities. Once again, the novelty of our latest idea seemed to wear off. Oh, how hard it is to be original!

Through all this we persisted with our research, determined not to waste one moment of it, particularly attendance at Melbourne Football Club and Collingwood Football Club functions. Eventually, about midway through 2001, it dawned on Penny (please excuse the pun) that that's what we should write about; simply our personal experiences of following football and our reflections on various aspects of supporting football. This angle underpinned our intention right from the start of the project, even in the first book proposal that comprised the birthday gift to Dawn all those years ago.

We were adamant that we didn't want to preach to people about the 'right way' to go about being a football fan, as each person's circumstances and experiences are unique. Rather, we wanted to share some of our stories in a way that expressed the impact that football has had on our day-to-day lives.

> Yes, we wanted to celebrate football from the perspective of women, not celebrate women as female football fans!

So what sort of a book is *Real Women Love Footy*? It is the accounts and thoughts of two women — us, no less! — who love football. It tells of our experiences with our clubs, maps the highs and lows of supporting our respective football teams, and honours the heroes who have given us so much pleasure and, no doubt, a reason for living! All right, the contents are obviously much more intimate and idiosyncratic to our individual histories and views of the world than they would be if we'd stuck with our earlier ideas. But we are confident that readers will relate to our stories in one way or another, if only to say, 'Oh, it's nothing like that for me!' Whether in agreement or disagreement with our perspectives, we hope to connect with or, at least, amuse people — especially women who are passionate about a sporting team.

So, here it is — *Real Women Love Footy*! Living proof that anyone can write a book about anything, and everyone has a story or two to tell. We hope you enjoy reading our stories as much as we enjoyed living them and writing about them.

Cheers!

DAWN LEICESTER & PENNY MACKIESON

Dawn: 'Penny, let go of Woey!'
Penny: 'No! We'll have to share him ...'

First Bounce

Autumn in Melbourne — mornings full of dew and sunshine, noon times that warm the soul, evenings that chill the bone. Rowers on the Yarra, Moomba in the gardens and the scream of racing cars in the streets. And football comes again.

The real thing's getting near after pre-season games that don't mean much. It's good when we win, not important if we lose. I check out new players, note the coach's latest moves and this year's new playing strip.

Excitement is growing as I start to get the kit together. I find my backpack and remember that I meant to have washed it last September. Plan the first trip — what will I take? It's too warm for a thermos, but remember to take water. I usually take sandwiches but buy lunch for the first match.

I know it only takes an hour to get there but still leave earlier than normal. The flutters have been there since morning and I can't wait to get to the ground. I get onto the train, with the paper and radio. Listen to the experts — who's going to win?

Crowds appear at Richmond station. I savour the moment and enjoy the walk towards the ground. Hear the boys and girls cry 'Record!'. Will I buy one now or wait? Nearly at the 'G'.

At the foot of the stairs I pause and look up in wonder. I feel the anticipation building as I start the climb. Look at the colour as two armies merge with one purpose.

At the turnstiles I present my ticket, virginal after the long summer break. Smile at the attendant, hand over my bag. Visit the loos — for once it's quiet. Now for my seat. It's early so there's plenty to choose from. The weather looks safe, so I try the open near the fence; it's good to hear what's going on.

There are two hours to go before the match but it's never a problem. I've got a book and there's plenty to see. I go to get lunch. The crowd is filling the ground. It's good to be early.

The cheer squads arrive. Start time is getting closer. They unroll the banners, add ropes — this one needs tape. Then up in the air as cheers fill the ground, like a salute, one way then another then back to the ground.

Suddenly an explosion! A team's on the ground. Get the banner up! They play the other team's song and I can't help singing. I hope no-one's watching and think, 'It's good to be alone!'

There's Bucks standing in front of his men — strong and controlled. Burnsie behind him then Rocca and Licca!

*J feel the lump start to swell and
J know why J'm here!*

The players hit the ground. They burst through the banners as the crowd erupts. 'The Premiership's a cakewalk' sung with full throat. It's been how many years? Don't remind me!

We've won the toss! Now last minute instructions and into positions. The sirens blow — less than a minute. The umpire raises the ball and sound explodes!

I'm almost numb with the force of thousands of people roaring, almost in pain. I know I'm a part of it but I'm almost hypnotised by the physical noise.

Whatever happens now is fate. We may win this one then win and lose so many more.

At the end of the day it doesn't matter!

Nothing will change it … it's in Me! It is Me!

It's football!

Going Alone
Life as a Solo
Football Supporter

Until the early 1990s, my involvement in football was fairly passive. I've been a Collingwood supporter since my first winter in Melbourne, but at the beginning my support was nominal at best. For the record, I was born in the UK and emigrated to Melbourne via Wollongong in 1972. I did go to the occasional game when I could persuade or bribe my father to overcome his aversion to all things Collingwood. While my passion for the game was gradually growing, I was forced to limit my enjoyment to the television set. Forced, yes, by my own misapprehensions.

Having said that, I did watch a lot of matches and events on television. Penny and I used to particularly enjoy the Brownlow Medal count and Penny was always convinced that Robbie Flower was robbed. The count turned into a real 'event' — which meant we drank a large amount of wine while we were watching it!

Who is Penny? Penny has been one of my closest friends since 1980. We met as students at Trinity College and in 1983 she was brave enough to volunteer to become my flatmate. A sign of our closeness is the fact that she is the only ex-flatmate that I still see — I don't know what that says about me? Penny is a passionate Melbourne supporter who has worshipped the red and blues from Barassi to Flower and now to Neitz. Penny has spent much time over the years protesting the general perception of Melbourne supporters as *hoity toity*. Strangely enough I've always considered that it was Carlton and not Melbourne supporters who were 'up themselves' — the silvertail image is hard for them to shake. Our friendship has also survived some horrendous Melbourne versus Collingwood games — but more of that later!

In 1983 I met and fell in love with Hugh, who I later married. Now Hugh is not a football fan. He nominally supports Essendon but when push comes to shove, I think he really has a soft spot for Collingwood. His passion is motorsport in which he was actively involved in our early years together. Because of his involvement, Hugh didn't really have time or inclination to watch other sports. Over the years, we've struck a compromise and I've taught him about my passions such as cricket, tennis and of course football and he's taught me about his. I've learnt a number of useful things, like:

- how to lap score in touring car races;

- when he tells you he'll arrange the best view at the circuit for you, he means 'get up the ladder and stand on the roof!'; and
- when you're travelling around a Grand Prix circuit in the back of a ute, it's a good idea to keep your legs in the car.

The most important thing he taught me, however, was not to expect a sensible answer in the week before he went to Bathurst. It's the equivalent to wanting a sensible answer at time-on in the last quarter of the Grand Final, with your team leading by three points and … well, you get the picture, I'm sure.

Football conversations in our house tend to have always been somewhat one-sided. I don't mind; I can talk for hours on the subject and it's only when Hugh starts snoring that I notice he's not listening. As a result of this indifference, there was little encouragement for me to do more than watch it on TV. From time to time I bribed Hugh with a dinner or something of that sort to take me to a game. One memorable occasion was when we didn't actually make it into the game. This was the Friday night when Collingwood played North Melbourne at the MCG and the MCC stuffed up the number of gates open for fans. There were thousands of people snaking in queues across the MCG car park long after the game had started. Hugh and I are not overly blessed with patience and after a quick reconnaissance we decided that a dash back home to watch the match on television was a good idea.

Another night saw Hugh and I with a group of friends brave the cold of a Melbourne winter to watch Collingwood play the Bears (the old Brisbane Lions) at the 'G'. As we made our way down Punt Road toward the ground, the famous clock on the silo showed not eleven degrees but six, and it was only 6.30 p.m. By the time the game started the temperature had dropped further and the wind was whistling around the mainly empty stands. There were about 16,000 fools at the ground that night — 15,850 Collingwood supporters and 150 frost-bitten Bears supporters — and I think we were all huddled together as much as possible. It's only when it's empty that you realise how bloody big the MCG is! Not surprisingly, the chilling experience quenched the little enthusiasm Hugh had for going to the football and he was less willing to attend. At this time, I was still labouring under the misapprehension that I needed someone else to go to the football with. And there's the rub you see; for years I believed that you couldn't just go on your own. It didn't occur to me that if I liked it, I should do it.

So we come to the next pivotal moment in my football life — 1990. Now, you all know why 1990 is so important to Collingwood supporters, but for me there was more to it than that. Part of the reason for this change was due to my meeting and becoming close friends with Tracey Walsh who, despite living in a house full of Carlton supporters, was as passionate a Collingwood supporter as you could ask for. We started going to matches together; not every week but a few in the year and more to the point, we both had someone in the office to talk to about football.

Now if you'll forgive me for diversifying here, this brings me to a very important point. As a woman, I am seriously frustrated at the lack of respect my educated opinion receives in football discussions! No, before you assume this is feminist soap-boxing, think about this scenario:

We are at a party on a Saturday night. That afternoon, Collingwood had played Geelong at Waverley Park and beaten them by a few goals. One of the highlights of the day had been a classic body on body battle between Gary Ablett and Gavin Brown. I had attended the match. During the party, three 'gentlemen' began discussing the day's results, including the aforementioned game. Always happy to have a yack about football, I joined in the conversation. Given that I was the only person present who had attended the game, I was absolutely dismayed when anything I said was totally disregarded and ignored. I tried on several occasions to give my eye-witness account of the match before giving up and walking away.

That incident occurred many years ago but the memory hasn't left me as similar incidents continue to this day. Why do men find it so hard to accept that women can enjoy and be knowledgeable about football and allow them to join in the office post-mortems?

Anyway, back to 1990. That year also marked my thirtieth birthday and I decided to celebrate it with a 'Black-and-White Party'. Hugh and I decorated the house with black and white streamers and balloons. Hugh arranged a black and white cake and all guests were asked to wear, you guessed it, black and white. I went in black and white but with an eye patch, which designated me as a 'one-eyed Collingwood supporter'. This soiree occurred on the last weekend of the home and away series and on a day when Collingwood finished the year with a crushing victory over North Melbourne at Waverley.

As the finals approached, the battle was on for seats and thanks to friends who were members we were able to attend most of the finals matches. We sat through the agony of the draw against the West Coast Eagles, then enjoyed the crushing wins over the Eagles in the replay and Essendon in the Second Semi-final. I even got Hugh to the last match, although it was one that he wished he'd stayed away from, surrounded as he was by two out of control Magpies supporters. Finally it was the big one, the Grand Final, the chance to atone for all those losses.

You can imagine my shattering disappointment at missing the Grand Final in person as I was unable to buy a ticket without resorting to a scalper. For the first time I realised that it would be better if I was a member not just a supporter! A sense of resolve began to permeate my dismay.

In late 1990, I finally woke up to the fact that I didn't need someone else to go to the football with; I was perfectly capable of going on my own. With trembling anticipation, I became a Collingwood member for the first time and planned my assault on the world.

I have to admit that the first time I went to a match on my own I was absolutely terrified. I was so sure that everyone was looking at me thinking that I was a complete loser for being there alone.

What I quickly discovered was
that I wasn't alone at all!

Sure, I wasn't there with someone in particular, but everyone at the ground was there because they enjoyed the game and a large percentage of them barracked for Collingwood — so what was I afraid of?

After my first couple of games, I grew more and more relaxed and was prepared to travel further afield. The greatest excitement of the year was my first game at Victoria Park, the spiritual home of the Black-and-White army. My visit coincided with the unfurling of the 1990 Premiership Flag and I have to admit to crying again as the roar of the faithful shook the ground. It was truly one of the most amazing moments of my life.

The other thing that struck me in that first year was the freedom that going alone gave me. Far from causing me problems, I actually came to relish those five hours or so of release from the responsibility of having to talk to someone. Sure, I would chat with people who sat near me, but I didn't have to! As I became more organised, firstly a Walkman and later a Discman became my companions and I loved the opportunity to absorb the sage comments of Tim Lane, Crackers Keenan and Dermott Brereton and to enjoy Eddie McGuire's passionate commentary. I once believed that I wouldn't be able to open my mouth when at the football alone — but I know now that this is ridiculous. I am a very vocal — but never abusive (well, occasionally abusive) — supporter and win, lose or draw I love the emotional and physical release of a day at the game. I liken it to primal

Dawn and Eddie; two passionate Collingwood supporters.

scream therapy and use it to release a huge amount of tension that builds up during the week.

Many people have expressed astonishment at my dedication to football going. The fact that I don't drive and live an hour out of the city seems to preclude me in their minds from having a life at all. I have never had a problem travelling around the city on public transport. Although I will admit that VFL Park had its own challenges, unlike the enjoyable trips to the MCG. I love going to Telstra Dome, which is so clearly set up for the public transport traveller. I have always drawn the line at travelling to Kardinia Park as the time it would take is somewhat prohibitive. (Can you imagine that journey home after a loss?) Night matches are also a problem. I won't travel on public transport at night so the only chance I have to attend these games is when someone agrees to go with me — this is where bribing Hugh comes in! It is the only restriction that I face but usually manage to get around it at least once a year.

In 1994, I became an AFL 'Restricted' Member; a decision made after experiencing the problems and cost of obtaining a seat at Collingwood's big MCG games. I now have the benefit of a seat on the wing and the use of excellent facilities. For the blockbuster occasions I am happy to arrive early in order to obtain a good seat and have no patience for those who arrive ten minutes before match time and complain. The best example was the 1995 Anzac Day Classic when Collingwood and Essendon met in front of more than 95,000 people. I arrived at 11.00 a.m. and had a brilliant position; eight rows from the front, right on centre wing.

After the match I saw footage of people crying because they couldn't get in. Well, most of them arrived at the last minute and expected to walk in and get a seat. They also complained about the preference given to both AFL and MCC members. May I say that we pay for that preference and have the right to it. Many of those who complain go to only one or two matches a year, while members are making a financial commitment to their clubs and to the competition and should be rewarded for this. Anyway, off the soapbox! That game on Anzac Day was an absolute privilege to attend. If there was ever a match that should be packaged and sold to convert the doubting, this was it. I have attended several drawn matches and felt frustration for one that got away, but on this occasion, it was the only fair result. Supporters of both teams shook hands at the end, all agreeing that they had witnessed a titanic struggle.

Queen's Birthday Matches:
Melbourne versus Collingwood

In recent years I've found myself enjoying a more social football experience as more and more friends have expressed an interest in coming along. Penny and I now have a traditional trip to the Queen's Birthday Collingwood versus Melbourne spectacular. (Well, okay, it's been three times, but traditions have to start somewhere.) I have to say that all games have been true tests on our friendship — only comparable to trying to get this book together.

Penny kindly invited me to take her six-year-old son Patrick's seat in the Melbourne area in 2000 and 2001 — not sure what Patrick thought of this, but thanks anyway. So picture this: me decked out in black and white, a passionate and vocal Magpies supporter surrounded by dozens of passionate and vocal Melbourne supporters. It makes an interesting social experiment and I can assure you that however nice they are to you before the game, it's a totally different story by three-quarter time.

In 2000 I had to endure watching the brilliant Jeff Farmer (sadly out of touch earlier in the season and for the first half of the game) turn on a stunning display in the second half and kick nine goals as Melbourne belted my Magpies. There is nothing worse than being surrounded by dozens of smug, rightly proud opposition supporters who are trying so hard to be nice to you — until they remember that you barrack for Collingwood then all efforts go out of the window — as they justifiably celebrate a sensational piece of individual and team dominance.

But I have a very long memory and I got my revenge at the 2001 encounter. On this occasion Collingwood, playing without Nathan Buckley, absolutely flogged Melbourne by 78 points and Chris Tarrant took the unofficial mark of the year. (Of course that's a totally subjective opinion but what the heck!) Now if opposition supporters have trouble being nice to you when they're winning, you can only imagine their efforts when their team is being pumped by the club they have long hated the most. It was hard for me — no, honestly! I love Penny and I hate seeing her upset. But it's hard not to be smug when your team is on top, especially given that we hadn't had a lot to cheer about for a few years. I tried to be quiet but the momentum got too much for me at about quarter-time and I let it rip! I'm lucky that Melbourne supporters are so civilised — not sure I'd have got away with it at Football Park!

Penny suffered again in 2002. On this occasion Patrick quite rightly wanted his own seat so I invited Penny to join me in the AFL Members and tempted her with lunch in the dining room. We had quite a party for this game as several other friends came along for what promised to be a top game. Both Melbourne and Collingwood were in the top eight and this spelled blockbuster! Someone forgot to tell the Melbourne boys that! Melbourne had the first five scoring shots of the match — and kicked five behinds. Then wouldn't you know it, Collingwood got the ball into their goal scoring area and kicked — five goals! The game was really over at that point; Tarrant went on to kick seven, while Josh Fraser had his best game of the season kicking four. Collingwood won by 51 points and Penny wasn't happy! In fact, she was really pissed off! I struggled to contain my glee in the face of her glowering expression and I'm sure her comments about the umpires were actionable. I had severe concerns about our ongoing partnership and friendship by the end of the game but I'm glad to say that her natural good humour returned shortly after.

The lure of the AFL Members' dining room, a bottle of red and a great seat is too much for some of my friends. I'm grateful for that because I've shared some magic moments with other passionate Collingwood supporters.

Ironically, one of the only matches that I went to alone in 2002 stands out above all others — yes, the last day in September, when Collingwood took on the Brisbane Lions and nearly scored a major upset. It was really strange. There I was, on a highly emotional day, and no-one to share it with! I had a great seat, three rows from the fence, near the fifty metre arc at the city end. Unfortunately, it was in the open, and as you'd all know, Melbourne turned on a filthy wintry storm that day! I was well wrapped up in a Driza-bone and rain poncho and had my trusty backpack wrapped in a garbage bag.

The good thing was that the guys on one side of me were ardent Collingwood fans. The bad thing was the guy on the other side of me was a real pain! I got all excited in the last quarter when Anthony Rocca unleashed that amazing goal (all right, it was a point!) and I leapt to my feet. All I got from the misery beside me was 'Sit down, I can't see!' Get a life, I say!

I didn't mind being alone — it's hard to feel isolated in a crowd of 91,000. I had lots of contact with the outside world (and with other supporters within the G) via my mobile phone. The SMS messages were flying, particularly during the quarter breaks. I have a friend who barracks for Brisbane (no, honestly!) and who was sitting high in the Northern Stand across the ground from me. We kept sending our comments across the ground — right up to three-quarter time. From then on, we were too busy biting our nails to do anything.

I did mind my solitude after Akermanis kicked what was to be the winning goal of the game. I knew that there wasn't time for Collingwood to kick two goals and that the dream of winning the 2002 flag would be just that — a dream. I held on until the end when I heard the final siren and saw the contrasting visions of elation and devastation and then saw Mick Malthouse's utter despair. And then I lost it. I stood with tears pouring down my face throughout the presentations and celebrations and the singing of the song and I've never felt so alone in my life. The phone had stopped ringing. It was as if the world outside had stopped. I couldn't wait to get out of the ground. Once on the train, I received a message from Hugh telling me of Mick's tears. I wrote back *Coming home. Please be kind!* He was.

Without going to the football I would have missed so much. I wouldn't have felt the elation of the 1995 Anzac Day game. I wouldn't have witnessed Mickey McGuane's amazing seven-bounce goal in 1993. I wouldn't have met the wonderful Magpie women who were such a big part of my years at Victoria Park. I wouldn't have stood silently sobbing at the amazing tribute to the late Darren Millane in 1992 or said goodbye to Ted Whitten on that emotional day in June 1995.

I wouldn't have been part of that amazing 2002 Grand Final where the team I love came so close to winning a historic victory. And I wouldn't have had the opportunity to be a part of the history of the Collingwood Football Club and to participate in something that means so much to me.

I am Melbourne, Very Melbourne!

I'm not known for my poetry, and with good reason! But I was pretty pleased with myself after writing *Footie Latte*; a poem that compares how much I need football with my other significant addiction — caffeine. I was so pleased with myself, in fact, that I thought I'd read it to Bruce, my husband. So I did, complete with the appropriate facial expressions and voice emphases. I was feeling very satisfied with my performance, and with myself in general ... that is, right up until I asked Bruce what he thought about my poem.

'Good, very Melbourne,' he responded.

'What do you mean, "very Melbourne"?' I asked, rather defensively.

'Oh, you know — very Melbourne Football Club ... very *Chardonnay*,' he elaborated.

Well! I was indignant, as I am every time Bruce — a Collingwood fan, born and bred — makes such a comment about supporters of my club! Ever since I've known him, since

1984, he has been making (what I interpret, at least) to be derogatory remarks about MFC supporters. He definitely gets at least some of his ideas from the Coodabeen Champions; he has confessed as much. He says things like:

> *They wear moleskins and tweed jackets with brown leather patches on the elbows, and they wear out their jacket elbows from too much 'bending the elbow' in the Long Room, you know?*

This comment invariably conjures up an image of ruddy skinned, red nosed, Western District graziers for me. But I figure those types would surely support Geelong Football Club, *not* Melbourne!

> *They're the ones who park their Range Rovers and Mercedes in the MCC car park.*

So what! Everyone has to drive something, and if you drive to matches you have to park your vehicle somewhere, don't you?

As for four-wheel-drives, well, I personally don't approve of driving them in the city. But if someone is going to have one it might as well be used for going up to the snow fields — most appropriate!

> *You won't see any Range Rovers in the car park during the footy season, though. They're all up at the snow in winter.*

It is an unfortunate coincidence of nature that the ski season happens to overlap significantly with the football season. I love skiing and, just for the record, so does the Collingwood fan in the house. Personally, I think it's a very difficult choice, though one made much easier as *we* can't afford to go skiing often. I'd go for two to three weeks every year if I could — so long as it didn't clash with my footy fixture, of course!

They're the Chardonnay set.

He's definitely got that wrong. Everyone knows that the 'Chardonnay set' is at Carlton Football Club. In any event, lots of people prefer drinking wine to beer, particularly women … and not just me! And lots of other people who drink beer also enjoy a wine too. It isn't exactly a crime, you know.

When they barrack they go, 'Rah, Dees!'

This one really gets up my nose; it positively winds me up like a tin soldier! I can honestly say that I have never, ever heard a Melbourne Demons supporter say, 'Rah, Dees!' when barracking at a match, let alone utter it myself! In fact, I don't think I've ever heard anyone with a decent plum in his or her mouth at the footy.

> *They're the ones with those little secret society stickers on their Range Rovers and Mercedes — you know, the little square navy coloured one with a red triangle pointing down and no writing on it?*

Secret society, pah! The fact that a Collingwood supporter knows what that sticker is all about means it is so obviously *not* a secret!

And what's wrong with putting your football club's sticker on your car? Members of all the other clubs do it, too (even the poo-coloured one that Hawthorn Football Club's got!).

*It's not like you have to pass
some sort of test or initiation rite to put a
membership sticker on your car — you
just have to fork over the money.*

Becoming a Melbourne Football Club member was very special for me and I couldn't wait to put my club membership sticker on my car. I was so proud. My car — that would be a Holden Vectra wagon, *not* a Range Rover or Mercedes — was brand new then. It is the only car I have bought new and I made sure it was navy, in keeping with my club's colours. (By the way, my previous car was a *red* Alfa Romeo 33 — cute as!)

I admit that around Kew, where we live, there are a surprisingly large number of vehicles with the red and blue MFC stickers on them. There are probably nine MFC-stickered cars for every other-stickered car representing all the other clubs put together, which truly astounds me given how close we are geographically to the home of the Hawthorn Football Club.

But anyhow, I didn't choose to support Melbourne because lots of other people in our suburb support them.

*I have been a fan of the Demons
since I was a kid in the country where it
wasn't at all cool to follow them.*

I didn't know Melbourne was supposed to be a 'rich man's club' until I went to university, and I didn't know I would be living in Kew until after I married Bruce — the *Collingwood* supporter!

Bruce's image of MFC members is, to my mind (and I sincerely apologise to all those people whom I may also have wrongly pigeonholed) an image of Melbourne Cricket Club members. That image is probably shared by many fans of other AFL clubs and probably by many MFC fans too. Of the 21,000 plus MFC members, over 3,800 (or about 18%) are also MCC members,[1] and the club believes 'there are in excess of 20,000 Demons supporters within the ranks of the MCC.[2] It is also worth noting that approximately 67% of MFC members are male,[3] with more than 60% of them aged forty or older.[4] These proportions differ significantly from the averages for the other AFL clubs; approximately 49% of the members of the other clubs were male with less than 30% of them aged 40 years or more in 1999.[5]

I may have an address that is 'typical' for an MFC supporter, and I probably even have a 'typical' MFC supporter family income — courtesy of Bruce the *Collingwood* supporter, I might add. However, I am definitely in the minority for gender and age group, and I don't belong to the MCC either. (The fact that I thought about joining my son up once and even got the membership forms sent out doesn't count, okay?) The bottom line is that I have never considered myself to fit the average profile of a MFC supporter and I don't believe I ever will, not while it closely resembles that of an ageing and conservative male bastion, anyway.

But whatever the average MFC supporter profile, why should I feel defensive about being a supporter of the oldest and most distinguished football club in the country? I'm not about to change the passion of a lifetime just because Bruce likes to make wise cracks about it. Well, 'Bruce' by name, 'Bruce' by nature, I say![6] I am very proud to be a member of the Melbourne Football Club ... end of story.

Well ... not quite. Attending my first MFC Member Information Night in 2001 really brought home to me the loyalty, passion and commitment I have for my club. The evening was very well presented, very professional — from being emceed by one of the club's favourite sons, David Schwarz, through the slides in club colours, right down to coach Neale Daniher's enthusiastic presentation towards the end. I was so inspired that first thing the next day I renewed Patrick's and my memberships by phone, and had the club send out membership packages to four other people who I knew were Demons fans but were not currently members of MFC.

What struck the biggest chord with me from that night, presented by MFC's Business Development Manager, Tim Gaspar, was the advertising slogan for the club for Season 2002 — *I am Melbourne*. Those three little words capture exactly how I feel about MFC, and exactly what I have been on about. Bruce can hang it on me as much as he likes, but the fact remains that I am Melbourne, I am Very Melbourne, and I am Very proud to be Melbourne! And I am proud to advertise my allegiance via the membership stickers on my car — particularly the little, square, navy sticker with the red triangle pointing downwards that is particularly legible for those who may have some difficulty reading!

Picking the Favourite

Open any footy survey from any source and you can almost guarantee that among the *which team do you barrack for? and how often do you watch football live/on TV/on the Internet/from the moon?* there will be the question *who is your favourite player?* It never ceases to amaze me that in such a team-driven sport there is such a fascination with individuals. I'm not setting myself up as anything different from the norm here; I know that my whole perspective of a team can depend on my opinion of one of their players. It's a fact that I liked the Adelaide Crows more when Mark Bickley was their captain because I felt he was a 'decent person' — almost a Victorian (just joshing!). Similarly, and much closer to home, I have far more respect for the North Melbourne Kangaroos now that Wayne Carey (Hiss! Boo!) has gone and that nice Anthony Stevens is in charge. Logical? Not at all. But it's a fact of life; our images of football teams and, to a far greater extent, footballers are based on raw emotions and instincts that are inexplicable to outsiders. My aim here is to share my observations on the process that causes an individual — and at times a crowd — to pick a favourite.

Childhood heroes

The process of picking your favourite player starts at a very young age. In football, traditionally, a child would have the number of his or her favourite player stitched onto their duffle coat or guernsey. Eddie McGuire often talks about how he hero-worshipped Peter McKenna and had the No. 6 on his back. Who can forget the response of young supporters every-where when, that icon of the Melbourne Football Club, Ron Barassi went to Carlton in 1965? When told of young children with No. 31 on their backs crying at the loss of their hero, the always sensitive President of Carlton, George Harris, was heard to reply that they could still wear No. 31 as Carlton would be giving him the same number!

As a child, my game was soccer and I was a huge fan of Manchester United. This choice was made so much easier by the fact that Georgie Best played for United. In the 1960s, Best rivalled the Beatles and other pop stars as a pin-up and I was mesmerised by his longish, dark hair, flashing Irish eyes and general gorgeousness. Of course I appreciated his football skills as well, but I think that was an afterthought.

My brother, Neale, didn't support United. For reasons that no-one in my family could understand, Neale was an Everton supporter. This was particularly hard for my mother's family as they were all Liverpool fans. To explain: both Everton and Liverpool are from, well, Liverpool, and theirs is a bitter rivalry — think Collingwood and Carlton but much, much worse. Anyway, Neale was an Everton supporter and the family had to hope he'd grow out of it. Part of Neale's fascination for Everton came from his favourite player, an English international by the name of Alan Ball. With no disrespect intended to Alan Ball (he was a fine player and a member of England's 1966 World Cup team) it's hard to see what the attraction was. Nevertheless, it was there and it was real. So real, that when Ball transferred to Arsenal in 1969, Neale, as a fickle seven-year-old, went too! The player in this instance was far more important than the team and Everton wasn't enough to hold Neale. I'm pleased to say that Neale saw sense when his hero moved again to lowly Southampton and decided to use another method to choose a team. He decided to go for the strength and success of — you guessed it — Liverpool, thereby ensuring years of happiness as he revelled in their success as well as full return to the ranks of the family.

The question of the importance of the player rather than the club was one that caused my co-writer, Penny, great consternation at the end of the 2001 season. Her concerns related to her son Patrick's favourite player, Jeff Farmer, who was traded to the Fremantle Dockers at that time. Of particular concern to Penny was the fact that Patrick had previously been a Dockers supporter (don't ask how, it was probably confusion from a passionate Melbourne supporting mother and a Collingwood-supporting father) and it had taken much persuasion (or brainwashing) on her part to convert him to the

Demon cause. How, she then feared, would Patrick respond to the loss of his favourite player to his previously favourite team? Thankfully for Penny, young Patrick showed a huge amount of maturity and loyalty and stuck with the Demons saying that it was a shame but that he'd just have to pick another favourite player. Interestingly, Paddy opted for Brad Green, No. 18, as his 'new favourite'. While not Melbourne's best player, he is certainly exciting and the reasoning is that he's young so he'll stay longer!

Nice legs — shame about the ...

It's inevitable, I hear you say, that a book about the experiences of women football supporters would eventually bring in the physical element. After all, according to many of the men we know, we women only attend football matches to 'ogle' at the boys in their shorts — not as tight as they used to be but so much more interesting. Let me just say that if I for one wanted to overindulge on the male form I could find a more comfortable location than the outer at the MCG on a cold and rainy Melbourne afternoon. If that isn't a recipe to dampen your ardour then I don't know what is.

Having said that, however, I also need to say that we are human as well as women (even though our husbands may not always agree) and that we are not unappreciative of the male form. Therefore, there is no doubt that physical perfection of some nature can play a part in choosing a favourite player. Interestingly, my extensive research has shown that faces are not as big a factor as other aspects of male anatomy.

My first example relates to my friend Kerry who is a

Brisbane girl, both the town and the club. She is a Lions member (curse her) and obviously loves all of her boys but like all of us, she has a favourite player. Now who do you think it could be? Could it be the devastatingly handsome Alistair Lynch: he of the wonderful cheekbones, those soulful eyes and elegant features? Or what about Nigel Lappin's almost Latin good looks? Or Michael Voss's 'every mother's favourite son' charm? No. The one that makes her knees tremble is the 'orange roughy' himself — Justin Leppitsch! I ask you! I've asked Kerry many a time what it is that makes her heart flutter and I usually get a giggle and an incoherent mumble — not something that you would actually expect from her, I can assure you. In a rare moment of lucidity on the subject, she told me that he had a great body, nice legs and all that. I said, 'But, what about the face?'

'Well,' she replied, 'he hasn't got the best head, but he looks fantastic from behind.' She has got a point. After all, a lot of football is viewed from behind the player so she'd have had ample opportunity to cop an eyeful — but, they don't make posters with back shots, do they? Mind you, I've noticed that even on the *Men for All Seasons* calendars some heads appear to be in shadow more than others!

Kerry's by no means the only fan I know with strange (to me) taste in what she finds physically attractive! I have another friend who was introduced to football by her partner. By the by, her partner is actually Canadian and has only been in Australia for a few years, while Sam is an Australian girl — go figure! Her partner, Patrick, is a passionate Hawthorn fan. Early in their relationship Sam couldn't give a hoot about any of it. She was persuaded, however, when Patrick took her to a

training session and she became aware of the physical perfection of — wait for it — Daniel Chick! Now I have nothing
personal against Daniel Chick, although I did wince when I
heard Hawthorn fans yelling out 'Chicky'. But he's not a pin-
up to me! Shane Crawford is a pin-up. Nathan Thompson's
pretty cute. Daniel Chick is a fine player, but in my opinion
he's got a head like a robber's dog. Not friendly I know, but an
effective comparison! In this instance again, I asked Sam
what the attraction was and gave my opinion that he was
homely to say the least. Strangely, she didn't disagree with me
but countered that he had a great body and that it was the
sight of it running around, gleaming with sweat that had converted her into a passionate Hawks supporter. I haven't seen
her since he was traded to West Coast. I wonder if she'll
change teams, or will she just lose interest!

It is a cliché, but it is true that beauty is in the eye of the
beholder and that what one person finds attractive will cause
another to shake their heads in disbelief. Penny and I, for
example, have argued long and hard about the differing
merits and attractions of the two Demons Davids; David Neitz
and the now retired David Schwarz. I have to admit that
Schwarz has been known to set my pulse racing! He's so big
and manly and has a lovely face. While Penny will wax lyrical
for hours over the virtues of the Melbourne captain — who, it
has to be said, does absolutely nothing for me. Similarly,
young Collingwood supporters go wild at the sight of Chris
Tarrant and Brodie Holland, while I look at them and think
'kids'.

There is no doubt that physical perfection is an important
factor in football popularity. Players such as Anthony

Koutoufides, Shane Crawford, Tony Modra and Ben Cousins are all fine exponents of the game. So, however, are Brett Ratten, Martin Pike, Mick Martyn and Damien Peverill, but you don't find best-selling calendars and posters featuring these players. The difference is glamour and physical attraction — and the more attractive you are, often the more popular you'll be.

Maternal instinct

I'm almost loath to raise this subject. It reminds me all too forcibly that I am reaching the age where many of my favourite players are young enough to be my children. It's true though, that as we get older, some women supporters view particular players in a maternal light and feel a need to protect them, probably from people like we used to be! Alternatively, for the older women, there are players that they hope their daughters will come home with one day. It's the 'every mother's favourite son' or Johnny Farnham syndrome!

I notice that mostly at Collingwood, with young players such as Paul Licuria and Josh Fraser. Women are terribly protective of these young guys — not withstanding the fact that the former is twenty-five years old and has won back-to-back Best and Fairest awards and the latter is now twenty-one and in his fourth season with the Magpies. Somehow, they both have an air of vulnerability and youth which brings out that maternal instinct. In addition, both boys are such nice guys that you can't help loving them.

Age is not necessarily a factor in the maternal love stakes. A prime example of this is the fiercely protective affection that women Demons supporters have for their former No. 5 David Schwarz. Football supporters everywhere are probably now familiar with Schwarz's moving story. His father was murdered in front of him when he was a child and he barely escaped himself. He has a fiercely loyal love for his mother, Mary, and she for him — and he's not afraid to tell the world about it! In addition, Schwarz returned from three knee reconstructions, facing the possibility that each of them could have ended his career. I think it's his commitment and his determination to give the game everything he's got that has made Schwarz so loved by Demons fans. I know two female Melbourne supporters well and they are almost evangelical on the subject. Penny black-banned *The Footy Show* for about a year after the infamous 'pie in the face' incident.[7] Any attempt by myself to view the incident as the joke that it was obviously intended to be was viewed as a lack of respect to a player who had suffered so much to come back to football. I realised at that point that this was one of those occasions where I could not understand Penny's perspective and that it was best I say nothing.

Am I guilty of the same narrow perspective? Absolutely. I can confidently say, in the case of the majority of Collingwood supporters, our man is Gavin Brown.

Brown, otherwise known as Rowdy, has been the beloved of Collingwood supporters everywhere since he started at the club back in the mid-1980s. He was the unlikely full forward in the Magpies' 1990 premiership year but is best known for being sensationally knocked out by Terry Daniher during the quarter-time melee. I can't speak for other supporters, but I can tell you that I jumped to my feet after the incident and called down the curses of all the fathers on Daniher and his family. Strangely, I didn't feel anywhere near as passionate when Daniher knocked out Craig Starcevich later in the game. I was angry, of course — but with Browny, it was personal. You couldn't hurt him! The fact is that Gavin Brown was one of the most courageous players ever to play the game and could certainly look after himself. Nevertheless, to the women of Collingwood he is a player to be protected and cherished. Woe betide an opposition player who was too physical with Gavin. The crowd would be up, full of indignation, telling the offender all about it.

Their fondness hasn't diminished with his retirement, either. One of the loudest and most heartfelt ovations at the 2001 Copeland Trophy Night wasn't for a winner, or even our beloved president. No, it was for a presenter — for Gavin Brown. And I swear that the eyes of the seven hundred or so women supporters there all softened as they looked at him.

I love you for your mind!

Loving a footballer for his mind seems like a contradiction in terms for many people and a waste of time for many more. It's my belief, however, that there is a place for intellectual and articulate footballers and that some women love them. This really shouldn't surprise anyone. Football supporters, like footballers, come in all shapes and sizes and there are many among the professional and business community who list football as their greatest passion. Therefore it's not unreasonable to believe that an educated, well-spoken footballer will be appealing to these women.

I know in my case that one of my earliest favourites was Mike Fitzpatrick — notwithstanding the fact that he was captain of my team's arch enemy, Carlton! Fitzy was a wonderful ruckman and a dual premiership captain, but it was his off-field image, with glasses and a business suit, that appealed to me. When I discovered that he was a Rhodes scholar, I was convinced that he was the man of my dreams — if only he'd change teams! Of course he didn't so I had to look closer to home for an intellectual soul mate.

I used to fancy Peter Moore. I'm not sure what, if any, his university qualifications were but he always struck me as a footballer who could string more than four words together without recourse to a dictionary and that's got to be a good thing! As I've always said, 'Looks are one thing but you've got to be able to talk to them afterwards!' At least Moore didn't look like he was a plumber or was going to end up running a pub (not that there's anything wrong with that!).

Similarly, I have a huge soft spot for Craig Kelly and he was for many years my second favourite Collingwood player; Gavin Brown was the first. Talking about brains and Craig Kelly in the same sentence used to inspire ridicule from many supporters. Let's face it, Ned was best known for his strong man techniques and actions on the field and not especially remembered for his erudite comments. Let's remember he was affectionately known as 'Cement Truck' by his team-mates. I took an interest after hearing him speak on *The Footy Show* when I realised that he spoke in an obviously educated manner and was able to produce a sentence that didn't include a string of 'you knows' — something of a rarity in a footballer, you know! It's been more as a former player that

Kelly has demonstrated his brains. He started and runs the hugely successful Elite Sports group which now manages many footballers and other sporting greats, as well as organising corporate and fan functions around major sporting events such as the Grand Final. On top of that, he's kind of cute as well; all in all, the perfect bloke for me — rich, successful, good looking and Collingwood Premiership player. What a shame he's got a wife and I've got a husband!

Love to hate!

It's inevitable, but we have to touch on this. On those surveys to which I referred at the outset, you are just as likely to be asked to name your least favourite player as you are your favourite. You've all been at games where someone has been roundly booed and catcalled by opposition fans — chances are you've joined in the process. Who are these players and what have they done to enjoy our enmity?

There are players who we've always hated and there are others who become dislikeable with time. In the first category, Wayne Carey stands head and shoulders above the rest. I have to say that I disliked Carey long before the dramas and revelations of 2002 and his ill-judged affair with Kelli Stevens. I've never liked him and I'm not alone there. While I certainly concede that he has been the dominant footballer of the past decade or so and has an uncanny ability to turn games in ten minutes of brilliance, at the same time I have to say 'I don't like him' and from talking to other women I learn that neither do a lot of others. Why don't we like him? Well, because he's arrogant, he's a bit on the dirty side, he cries to the umpire if something goes against him and he's a chauvinist pig! Women, however, are strangely sanguine about the whole Kelli Stevens affair with most of those I've spoken to taking the view that it takes two to tango and she's as much to blame as he is.

Other great players who have copped the wrath of opposition supporters include Collingwood's own Nathan Buckley (I remember a time when even Magpies supporters were hostile to him), Greg Williams and even Gary Ablett. It would be too easy, though, to say that supporters hate them because they're good. Few people ever boo James Hird, Andrew McLeod or (in my opinion, the best footballer going around) Michael Voss. So there has to be more to it than that.

Some players start out as crowd favourites but become pariahs. One example is the recently retired Tony Liberatore. When he won the Brownlow Medal in 1990, the football world lauded 'Little Libba' and his fighting qualities. Media and fans alike loved and admired him. By the time he retired midway through the 2002 season, he was reviled and disliked by all except Bulldogs fans. Why? Because his style of play was perceived to be dirty and directed at the man and not the ball. This may be horribly unfair, but, as a colleague said to me recently, 'Perception is reality to many people', and we perceived him to be dirty and therefore didn't like him. Other players to start off as heroes and end up as villains include Gavin Wanganeen; another Brownlow Medallist who is now seen as a slightly suspect player who stages for free kicks. Jason Akermanis is another example of a player who's going the wrong way in people's minds. When Aker won the Brownlow in 2001, I was amongst many supporters who cheered and thought it was wonderful. I liked the way he played and the sense of fun he brought to both the game and the way he celebrated it. By the time the 2002 season had finished, I was sick to death of him and could not bring myself to say a kind word about him. He's opinionated and conceited and turning into a thoroughly unpleasant character. I know this feeling is widespread because I've had a number of people call me since the Grand Final and tell me that Licuria should have got three weeks for not stomping on his head!

He's my favourite!

I've discussed reasons for making one player a favourite but not answered the question *who's my favourite player at the moment*? As you have seen, I've had a few favourites over the years. Starting with Peter Moore and Rene Kink, moving through to Craig Kelly and my all time number one, Gavin Brown. But what of the current crop?

It's often assumed that Nathan Buckley has the honour. But, while I certainly say that he's the best player at Collingwood — and one of the best in the competition as a whole — he's not my favourite. Who is?

Well, it's fair to say that I do think Jarrod Molloy is a breathtakingly attractive person who has been known to reduce me to absolute gibberish at the thought of speaking to him! So if I were going for looks alone, it would be Molloy.

And, I really have a soft spot for Paul Licuria. He is not only devastatingly good looking and a fantastically underrated footballer, but also a truly nice person who is liked and admired by everyone I've spoken to at the club.

Also, as Penny will tell you, I'm terribly protective of Anthony Rocca and have been telling people for years that he would be a great footballer and confirm all that potential — and anyone who watched the 2002 Grand Final would have to agree with me!

Finally though, there is one player who seems to click on so many levels. He's talented, he's cute, he's intelligent and has interests outside of football, and he brings out the latent mothering instinct in me. It's Rupert Betheras and I love him.

Me and my Rupe.

I first noticed him because of his name — even I have to admit it's unusual. Then I read about how his acceptance speech, when he was named the Best Reserve Player, so moved new president Eddie McGuire with his passion and commitment to the club. Then I saw him play and thought 'wow'. He's not the most talented player out there and he seems to sneak under the opposition's guard but he'll pop up and do something special when it counts. If you don't believe me take a look at Collingwood's three biggest wins of 2002, Round 8 against the Lions and the two finals wins, and you'll see Betheras goals at key moments. Rupert sealed his spot in my affection when I had the opportunity to meet him at a Women in Black players' function in 2001. We had our photo taken together and he was so warm and friendly and interested that that was it for me. When he was on fire in the third quarter of the 2002 Preliminary Final and the crowd cheered 'Rupe! Rupe!', I was as proud as punch. Rupert, your No. 10 will be on the back of my metaphysical duffle coat from now on!

Facing the Ferals

I need to state right up front that Collingwood supporters have a well-deserved reputation for being fiercely loyal, vocal, passionate and probably unpleasant, depending on your football perspective. Similarly, all other clubs have a percentage of supporters who make even their fellow fans cringe. I have particularly nasty memories of Carlton supporters who, amongst other things, have entertained themselves by throwing things at my hat or spitting at me. Having said all that, for full-on feral behaviour — particularly on their own turf — nothing can beat the Adelaide Crows supporters.

The Croweaters have always believed that theirs was the competition that mattered, naming their league the South Australian National Football League — a misnomer if there ever was one! They also believed, with some justification, that Victorian teams were marching to greatness by stealing the best young players from across the border. South Australians yearned to put the best of their state in direct competition with the Victorian teams. Similarly, the administrators of the newly named AFL, who had seen teams join from Queensland and Western Australia and established a franchise in New South Wales, knew that the competition could not be truly national without representation from South Australia. After many shenanigans involving the Port Adelaide Magpies, it was announced that a new team would join the league in 1991. This was the birth of the Adelaide Crows!

My first experience with Crows supporters was in their inaugural year. To put things into perspective from a Collingwood point of view, it was Round 14. Collingwood were suffering from a major premiership hangover, had earlier lost six consecutive games and were in serious danger of missing the finals. Things had improved slightly with a fighting win over Essendon in Round 12, followed by a thumping 99 point win against the Sydney Swans. The next opposition to be faced were the brand-new Adelaide Crows.

I have to admit that the Sydney win was an early sign that the Collingwood players had woken up and were playing the type of football that had taken them to the flag the year before. I was sufficiently confident about the forthcoming game that when asked during the week what I thought the result would be, I confidently predicted that the Pies would prevail by ten goals. At this point there were howls of derision from everyone within earshot. I was sure though. I'd seen the boys and I knew. I even accepted wagers on my claim so we had to win — otherwise I was down three Quick Picks and a few bottles of champagne. Anyway, I felt that we had a state responsibility.

After all, there were plenty of early reasons to dislike the

Crows; they had slightly dorky stripes (the navy, red and gold was never figure enhancing and made me think of overgrown bumble bees); there was the ongoing State of Origin history; they were cocky and from South Australia. Having said all that, you actually had to feel a little sorry for the innocents from the City of Churches who presented themselves at Victoria Park that winter afternoon. Well, almost! There were early signs that the Crows' hierarchy were aware of the dangers of facing a resurgent Collingwood at Pie Park. Crows coach Graham Cornes ordered a training run for his players at 9.30 a.m. on the morning of the game. History shows that this wasn't a winning move!

My first year of Club membership was in 1991 and at that stage I didn't have a regular seat at Victoria Park. As a result, I used to organise a seat once I got to the ground as I'm not dedicated enough to consider standing in the outer for a match. This usually took me to the lower section of the Rush Stand which is just to the right of the Social Club stand and the area usually allocated in part to the visiting cheer squad. I'd sat in this section at several other home games without a problem. I loved the close proximity to the players (my seat was often in the front row) and had sat with other like-minded Magpies fans in the past. On this occasion, however, things were to be very different.

As I walked to my seat, I noticed the largish contingent of Crows supporters to my left and realised that this was indeed their cheer squad. Thinking that this could make things interesting, I looked for my seat ready to have a chuckle with my neighbours at their expense. I was, again, seated in the front row next to a youngish (well younger than me) couple who, beyond wearing dark coloured clothes, showed no visible signs of support for either team. Assuming that they were Magpies supporters, I made an opening remark such as, 'There're a few bloody Crows here today. Hopefully we can give them a miserable trip home.' Not kind, I know, but nothing compared to what I could have said. (Now, what's the definition of 'assume'? It 'makes an ass of you and me!' Behold the ass!) Imagine my horror when they both smiled at me and produced Crows scarves! 'You're not, are you?' I croaked. He nodded gently with a slightly glazed, fanatical look in his eyes and waved his hand, indicating, 'We all are!' I looked around and with dawning horror realised that I was totally surrounded by Crows supporters! To put this into context, there were probably at most a few hundred in among some 28,000 Collingwood supporters. But when you are one among that few hundred, it's more than a little daunting.

Not being the brave type, I sat down quickly, apologised for any offence and buried myself in my lunch, my record and anything else I could find. I also looked around for an adequate escape route, finally deciding that the best option would be over the fence onto the ground! Desperate stuff indeed! Despite my concerns and opening gambit, things settled down for a while as we waited for the real thing to start. I eventually relaxed sufficiently to take account of my surroundings and to peruse the opposition more closely.

Looking at the cheer squad, two things were immediately apparent; they hadn't had much sleep, and they had made up for it by consuming a great deal of beer (or other such substances!). This had the potential to get ugly, either at the ground or on the bus home — and I prayed that it was the latter! The cheer squad was in full voice early. They roared out encouragement for their team and piled derision on their opponents — very brave given their location, and positively terrifying given mine! The appearance of the Crows onto the ground brought a guttural roar from the faithful few as they sang the club song with fervour. The subsequent appearance of the black and white heroes brought an even more fervent response from the visitors. As if to compete with the cheers of support and anticipation from the Magpie Army, the Crows boys and girls gave their own commentary. In a nutshell the Collingwood team were pretenders, Shaw was weak, Manson was a girl and Kelly was a cement head (well, a few Magpies supporters may have agreed with that one). And what of your fearless correspondent, I hear you ask? What was I doing during all of this? Well, I have to tell you, I decided that discretion was the better part of valour, so was intending to stay quiet. You guessed it, it didn't happen! I couldn't help myself. The Black-and-White warriors ran past and I clapped and cheered, I sang the song and cheered again — then I sat down and tried to look invisible!

As the match started, I promised myself that I would stay quiet. I wouldn't provoke the visitors any more. Okay, so that lasted about ten minutes into the first quarter! The match was an absolute hammering by the mighty Magpies with the final result being a whopping 23.22.160 to Adelaide's paltry 5.7.37. One thing I noticed about the Crows supporters is that their support lasted about as long as any chance of a real contest. In other words, it had diminished by quarter time. Up to that point they were cheering and supporting and encouraging, but the reality of the situation hit early and this stopped.

Don't worry, they didn't stop making a noise, it's just that the encouragement stopped and the abuse started.

For the next two quarters, I heard an increasingly garbled commentary on the sexual and other personal habits of the Collingwood players and coach that would make your hair curl. I would have been grievously offended had I not been so excited by what was happening on the field and on the scoreboard. Even the abuse had run out of steam by the last quarter and the combination of beer, lack of sleep and disappointment took its toll on the visitors. I looked around and saw that most of them were in a comatose state, staring blankly at the ground with looks of disbelief. One or two hardy souls swayed and told anyone that cared to listen (i.e. no-one) that it would be different next year when they welcomed us to Football Park. As you can imagine, there wasn't a huge care factor about next year among the Magpies fans within earshot — 'Scoreboard!' was their response.

At the end of the game I sang the song a couple of times and clapped and cheered the boys off the ground. I then gathered my things ready to head for the train. By this time I had pretty much forgotten my fear of the visitors and was quite relaxed as I headed for the exit. Those supporters who were still in their seats were slumped, exhausted by the experience. I noticed many others were already on the bus outside the exit — obviously it was more comfortable to sleep there. I thought, these Crows supporters don't seem too scary to me. How wrong I was to be!

As years went by, my involvement with the Crows supporters was a distant affair. For the record, to the dismay of their loyal supporters, Collingwood won both encounters in

1992, including their first visit to the dreaded Feral — I mean Football — Park. I went to several games, firstly at Victoria Park and later at the MCG, but managed to avoid close contact by sitting safely among my own kind. I did, however, hear increasingly ugly stories about the nature of the people of Adelaide, particularly in their reaction to Victorians. Opposition fans would visit Football Park and come away somewhat shell-shocked and vowing never to repeat the experience. I have even heard strong men say that they'd sooner face the infamous Animal Enclosure at Moorabbin rather than take on a Footy Park crowd again.

The scariest expression of anti-Victorian sentiment was the vandalism of a car parked in the official Football Park car park because it had Victorian number plates — trouble is it belonged to the Crows coach Robert Shaw! I blame Jeff Kennett for the trouble. Honestly! Since he 'stole' the Grand Prix from Adelaide there's been nothing but trouble. South Australians used to be really welcoming and friendly to Victorians, but it all changed.

Just as an example, in 1986 Hugh and I went to the Australian Grand Prix in Adelaide. We were pressed for time and parked in a fifteen-minute car park — for four hours. As we made our way back to the car, we noticed that a lot of the cars had tickets. 'Great,' we thought, 'this is going to make it an expensive trip!' Then we noticed that it was only South Australian cars that had tickets. Any car with interstate registration was let go. How friendly is that? Anyway, now you think twice about taking your car into South Australia, much less over-extending your welcome in a parking space and it must be someone's fault so I'm blaming Bloody Jeff. But I digress!

In 1998 I went to my first MCG Grand Final. I was fortunate enough to be invited on a corporate jaunt and had a splendid day which started at the famous North Melbourne breakfast and then included a river cruise for lunch before climaxing at the MCG in great seats for the decider. The North Melbourne Kangaroos were red-hot favourites for the Premiership, despite the fact that their opposition, the Adelaide Crows, were the reigning premiers. I found it hard to get enthusiastic about either team — I've never been a huge fan of North Melbourne and the thought of the cup going across the border again was almost too much to contemplate. On balance, I was slightly on the side of the Melbourne team but you wouldn't say that it was heartfelt support. To trot out a cliché, all I was hoping for was a good, tough, close game.

What I got, of course, was a tight first half during which the Kangaroos managed to blow their chance to post a match-winning score by kicking inaccurately, followed by the rampant Crows running amuck in the second half and winning by a comfortable margin. I enjoyed watching the silky skills of Darren Jarman and the magical qualities of Andrew McLeod — honestly. What I didn't enjoy was being seated behind the Adelaide Cheer Squad or the repeated renditions of the Crows theme song. I swear that if I'd had to sit through another version of 'We're the Pride of South Australia', I couldn't have been accountable for my actions. Just on the Crows' club song, I have to say that while I appreciate the partisan nature of these songs and their strange lyrics, which are a result of trying to get words to fit the music, I think the

Crows are asking for ridicule by including the line 'admiration of the nation'. Really, I can only assume that the 'nation' is the same one that competes in the South Australian National Football League!

The thing driven home to me that day was that, apart from having the most irritating club song in the competition, the Crows supporters are essentially fair-weather ones. That is, they are silent when their team is down and behind, but incredibly vocal when it looks like they might win. I'd certainly noticed that in my initial encounter at Victoria Park but I'd put that down to nerves at their foreign surroundings and the fact that they weren't in the game from the first bounce. Other Collingwood–Adelaide matches I've attended have been quite close-fought affairs but the Crows supporters were in the minority so it wasn't so obvious. It was very clear, though, in the 1998 Grand Final. The Crows supporters may as well not have been there during the first half when the Kangaroos were in the ascendant, but they certainly made their presence felt during the second half as the Crows got on top. Obviously they were resting their voices earlier in the match — don't want to peak too early you know!

I have to say I was prepared to forgive this silence and lack of support from Crows supporters as I'd only ever encountered them on the road, i.e. away from Football Park. I figured that they might feel overwhelmed or out-numbered and unwilling to make a lot of noise in case life was made difficult for them. It would be really different when they played at home, I thought.

Actually, it's worse when they play at home. There are so many of them and so few opposition supporters that the silence is scary. I've been to Football Park twice, to see Collingwood play the Crows, and Collingwood play Port Adelaide Power. My team lost narrowly on both occasions and I really got to see the ugly side of football supporters, from the most unlikely people.

I've talked about the circumstances of my first trip to Footy Park in *Football, Dad and Me* and explained what a hair-raising event it was for my poor dad. Let me tell you that it was no picnic for us visitors from Victoria either. Believe it or not it started at the pre-match dinner. We attended the Collingwood function and after a good feed, sat back to enjoy a talk from former Magpie great and proud South Australian, Murray Weideman. I can't remember the details of Murray's talk but he was obviously geeing up the Maggies who were in the middle of a disastrous year which was to result in the 'winning' of the wooden spoon for only the second time in their history.

What I do recall, however, was Murray being heckled by a smooth-looking type at one of the tables who was wearing (you guessed it) an Adelaide Crows jacket and scarf. Now, I don't care who you support, but this 'gentleman' was a guest of the Collingwood Football Club and showed an amazing lack of common courtesy in his behaviour. He was quickly shushed by his friends — who must have been wondering why they'd invited him — but sat smiling smugly throughout the rest of the talk. I didn't notice him once we got to our seats; I was far more interested in our prime location — with the Collingwood Cheer Squad — and the game.

The match saw a tight first quarter and then Collingwood

getting on top in the second and third quarters before the Crows ran over them in the last. During the first quarter, we noticed the presence of the Football Park 'roar meter' which measured the noise after each Adelaide goal — phew, that was exciting!

There was a lot of noise from the Adelaide supporters in the first quarter and the teams went goal for goal. The mood changed in subsequent quarters as Collingwood dominated the scoring — it seems that the only noise was for a Crows goal — no barracking to be heard otherwise! It was quite eerie as the only noise seemed to be coming from the 1000 or so Magpies faithful who had made the trip interstate. We'd cheer goals, encourage good passages of play and kept up a constant barrage of Collingwood! clap, clap, clap! Nothing from the Crows unless they scored a goal — so not much then for a large part of the game.

That all changed in the last quarter as the Adelaide team started to run down and overtake the gallant Magpies unit who had given everything they had. As the Crows piled on the goals, the noise level increased significantly, including comments between goals and not just responses to them. And this was what was so unpleasant about them. I've said it before about supporters of all breeds — sadly even to Collingwood supporters on occasions — but you're there to support and encourage your team and not to heap abuse on the opposition (well, not unless you're absolutely forced to!).

Unfortunately the Crows supporters didn't understand that.

Once they were pretty sure they were going to win, the abuse started.

And this wasn't just directed at the players. No. The comments about the intelligence, parenthood and criminal tendencies of the small Magpies contingent were also coming thick and fast.

I have to admit that I found their abuse very difficult to ignore and that it was only Penny muttering 'Don't lower yourself to their level, Dawn' that kept me from giving them a spray in return. One young Magpies supporter wasn't so lucky and, driven to total frustration by the inevitable defeat of his team and the slanderous comments being heaped on him, he snapped and turned to confront his tormentors. I can swear that he didn't lay a punch on anyone, just grabbed a lapel and gave them some home truths — then it was on! Other Crows supporters started to jostle and Magpies cheer squad members waded in to protect their own. The arrival of the security guys put an end to the trouble, and an end to the game for one chastened Magpies supporter, but it did nothing to remove my feelings of disgust and unease. I turned around to identify the perpetrator and saw, settling back in his seat and smiling broadly, the same smug bastard that had heckled Murray Weideman at the Collingwood function! Now I'm not a violent person — honestly — but I was desperate to wipe the smile off his face. Years later, I'm still angry about the night. I find it disgusting that a professional, mature man could take such pleasure in tormenting a young man whose only crime was to support his team. Even my dad, a Crows supporter, thought the whole thing was on the nose!

Collingwood lost the game by less than a kick after a Rupert Betheras mark on the goal line was disallowed and a free kick paid to Adelaide. It was hard for Magpies supporters to swallow after coming so close to an upset victory (as was the running commentary from Crows supporters as we left the stands). I was still seething from the earlier incident and this anger was fuelled as my proud club was pilloried by these South Australian Johnny-come-latelys! After being told to 'F*** off back to Victoria, you f***ing Collingwood c***!' (and this from a woman by the way!) I nearly lost it and had to be physically restrained by the ever-faithful Penny, while Dad gallantly shepherded the three of us out of the line of fire.

After calming down over a stiff brandy at the post-match function, I asked Dad about the strange supporter behaviour; the reactive rather than proactive crowd noise. His belief is that it stems from the fact that the Crows are a new franchise and that until 1991 all of their supporters were previously supporters of other clubs. Also, while Port Adelaide is deemed the 'working class' team in Adelaide, the Crows appeal to the Chardonnay set who enjoy the victory and the spoils of winning, but don't like doing the hard work to get there. I wonder then if this will always be the case with Crows supporters or whether there will be a generational change in another four or five years when their members will have been born Crows supporters — it will be interesting to see.

It's been some years since that night but the memory still burns in my brain. I've seen Collingwood beat the Crows a few times since then — most significantly in the 2002 Preliminary Final — and I've always been conscious of the fans and what they're going through. Last year I went back to Football Park to see the Pies play Port Adelaide Power. Again, it was a tight match played against a fiercely parochial crowd, but that's where the similarity ends. The Power supporters are from a traditional base and have loved Port Adelaide all their lives, and it shows. They cheer and encourage the good play and groan and despair with the mistakes. Yes, they gave heaps to my boys and especially to former Port Adelaide Magpie Nathan Buckley, but this is only what a Collingwood crowd would do so I could forgive it. Hell, before the advent of the Power most of them would have supported Collingwood, so why should I complain? I'd go back to Footy Park for a Port game, but I'll need a lot of convincing to go back to see the Crows.

Champagne Football
Life in the Social World

Seeking 'the total football experience'

If 'racing is the sport of kings', football is the sport of queens. That's right! Week after week, we female fans get to watch dozens of elite, young male athletes putting their incredible skills (*not* to mention their incredibly buff bodies) on the line in the context of a picturesque arena, and from where else but the comfort (albeit relative) of the stands. Not only that, but we are allowed to be as vocal and as demonstrative as we like (well, almost) in supporting our team during a match. In fact, the louder the better because teams love to have the supporters 'behind them' and the players really respond to a parochial crowd — the whole point of a home ground advantage, no doubt.

It doesn't end there, of course.

Anything worth doing is worth celebrating later.

So, for devotees of the sport of queens, this means après football functions, which provide a perfect opportunity to dress up (and I mean *new* frock, *new* shoes, *new* bag, *new* hairdo, and the rest!). On getting dressed up (or 'trussed up' if it's a black tie affair, and that's certainly when I feel most regal) we then get to drink up and (best of all!) schmooze up to our favourite players.

I always admired Dawn for having joined her club so many years ago, and attending matches usually on her own. But now when I look back, it was obvious that Dawn would get so worked up (as do most ardent football supporters) at a match, let alone a whole season of them, she really needed another forum to reward and normalise her emotional investment. It seemed like she was part of a big family (everyone has heard of 'the Collingwood army', haven't they?) but didn't participate in any of the family celebrations or commemorations related to milestones and significant events, like being hatched, matched or dispatched!

Conversely, I now see that, until I actually joined up as a member of Melbourne Football Club, I had pretty much always enjoyed my football somewhat voyeuristically; occasionally live from the stands, but more often than not via television or radio. In many ways I guess I tried to avoid getting too worked up about my footy team's performances.

But once I took the plunge and committed myself to joining up for season 1999, I made a conscious decision that I wanted (maybe even needed) 'the total football experience'. I was seeking to enjoy the social side of my club membership as well as the obvious match attendance role. I wanted to have my cake and eat it too. As I knew no other MFC members at the time, it was clear that I was either going to have to make some new friends pretty fast *or* convince my old friends that they would enjoy attending my club's social functions with me (even if they were members of other clubs or, for that matter, weren't even especially interested in footy — heaven forbid!). I basically opted for the latter, though, in the process of discussing and attending various MFC functions, I have also made some wonderful new friends within the club.

Dawn, I must say, embraced my approach with much enthusiasm. She was equally keen to attend social functions for both my club and hers. We made a pact to accompany each other to the functions of the other's choice, and invite (or drag!) along as many of our friends as we could. So, it was with great expectation that I organised tickets through MFC and subsequently went to my first 'champagne football' function. It wasn't an 'après football' function as such because it was actually held *prior* to the Melbourne versus Port Adelaide match on Saturday, 24 April 1999.

The occasion was the MFC President's Lunch held at the MCG. Oh, yes! I remember it well (mainly because I wrote down notes immediately on getting home that evening). It also happened to be the first official function that members of the newly formed Women of Melbourne coterie had been invited to. I had no idea I would join this group when I phoned MFC in 1998 to get a membership application. A flyer arrived in the same envelope and I thought to myself, 'What great timing! The girls *will* be impressed!' Of course, I invited my friends, Dawn (a Collingwood member) and Rhonda Ferguson (a long-time Carlton supporter) to be my guests at the function … and to hold my hand!

We made a point of introducing ourselves to Ann Sherry, the Chairperson of the coterie, and couldn't resist doing a bit of celebrity spotting; we saw Anthea Crawford and Perri Cutten (fashion designers), Nicky Buckley (model, TV presenter, and Demons convert) and her husband, Murray Bingham (model, TV presenter, and Demons converter), and Allan Stockdale (former Treasurer of the Government of Victoria). Garry Lyon, out of the team that day with an injury concern, was the guest speaker at the lunch, standing in for Joseph Gutnick who was then the MFC President and, of course, not available to attend any functions (football or otherwise) held on Saturdays due to it being his Sabbath. The only spoiler for the day was that the emcee kept calling the Women of Melbourne coterie members 'ladies' in a way that made it sound like the sign on a toilet designated for females.

But we were triumphant — we had actually done it! Dawn and I had attended our very first football-related social function. It was quite exhilarating, actually, and not as scary as we had anticipated. I admit that it was a bit surreal, eating our lunch at a table so close to people that we had only ever seen previously on television or in newspapers and magazines, but we felt that we adjusted pretty quickly (we only pointed and giggled once — just kidding! … It might have been twice.)

Looking back on it, I think the best thing about that first function was there being so few current footballers there — in fact, probably just the one, being Garry Lyon. It was good for us because we didn't have to battle the excessive shyness and nerves that we now know can be associated with being in the presence of a multiplicity of one's current heroes.

Obviously we wouldn't have expected players who were about to participate in a match to attend a pre-match function.

Of course, we've been to oodles of football-related social functions, both together and separately, since that first President's Luncheon. The Collingwood functions have included: pre-match and post-match events, including some interstate; a Women in Black coterie event, and a breakfast; a fashion show and a number of best and fairest dinners. The MFC functions have included: an intimate Women of Melbourne lunch and match viewing from Joseph Gutnick's private box at the MCG; a black tie Testimonial Dinner for the recently retired Jim Stynes; the MFC Team of the Century Dinner (also black tie); several Women of Melbourne luncheons; a pre-match function and a best and fairest presentation.

Schmoozing Jim Stynes at his Testimonial Dinner, 1999.

The 'I can't do that!' syndrome

There has, of course, been an abundance of current players present at many of the football club functions we have attended, hence our discovery about having to battle debilitating shyness, in Dawn's case, and nervous attacks, in mine, in order to get an autograph from or photograph with our favourites. Dawn keeps saying that I have 'more front than Myers!' But I know I don't (for the record, I'm a size 14C). What I do know is that the occasions to which Dawn is referring are functions to do with *her* football club, when I have been unaffected by the presence of the players as they were *her* heroes rather than mine.

For me, there is nothing more empowering than accompanying my shy friend to a function of her choice with the goal of ensuring that she leaves the function fully satisfied and, therefore, has been able to schmooze up to her favourite players. Give me a mission, and I'm on for it (and let's face it, I'm not about to pay good money for a ticket and go to the trouble of tarting myself up just to retreat into a corner like a wallflower — no way!). One of my most successful strategies when accompanying Dawn to a football club event is that, first, we both deploy some Dutch courage. I then keep an eye out for the players Dawn wants to get up close and personal with, wait until their personal queue of fans has thinned somewhat, and then say to Dawn, 'Hey, there's Rupe (or whoever)! Let's get him!'

At this stage, the colour of Dawn's face has been known to drain away, and she invariably responds, 'I can't do that!' Of course I understand that she doesn't *feel* like she can do it, but

I take very seriously my responsibility (albeit self-appointed) to ensure that she *does* do it. So, I always say to Dawn, 'Oh, yes you can!' Then, before she has a chance to dwell on her shyness any further, I literally drag her towards her idol and, armed with a camera, say something innocuous to him like, 'My friend is a great fan of yours and would *love* to have her photo taken with you — would you mind?' Of course, they never *do* and hey, presto! Dawn gets her photograph (assuming I've not had too much Dutch courage prior to then and manage to keep their heads lined up and focused within the frame).

The strength of this strategy is, of course, sometimes also its weakness. Reliance on a confidence booster that is wet and bubbly has obvious pitfalls. For example, take the Women in Black post-match function I attended with Dawn in 2001 at Colonial Stadium (now Telstra Dome). Collingwood had soundly defeated the West Coast Eagles in a night match. It was quite some time until the players emerged from their showers and light after-match meal (mind you, none of the Magpies supporters in over-abundance seemed to notice!). Dawn and I were forced to fill in time at the bar — I can't quite recall how many Ruskies we had consumed before we spied any of the players. I do, however, remember approaching many of Dawn's heroes on her behalf (maybe with the exception of Jarrod Molloy — hubba, hubba!) with great gusto later that evening, and getting lots of great photos of her with them. That was the good bit.

The not so good bit was when I approached the Magpies captain, Nathan Buckley, who had not played in the evening's victory due to recovering from an injury. I was on a roll so, with Dawn in tow behind, I bowled up to Buckley when the coast was reasonably clear (that is, when the throng of young female groupies had thinned). Feeling very confident by this stage, I ventured a new line of chitchat while engaging Buckley to autograph something for Dawn and pose with her for the mandatory fan photo. 'Well, Nathan,' I said, 'the boys played so well tonight I can't see there being room for you in the side next week!' Well, if looks could kill, I would have needed CPR! You would have thought I was Mick Malthouse and I had just told Buckley, 'Mate, your career is over, you'll never play for this club again!' The filthy expression on Buckley's face — it was almost enough to burst my confidence bubble, and definitely more than enough to drive me back to the bar for another Ruskie (or was it two?). Buckley went on the next week to play an absolute blinder of a match, according to Dawn. She reckoned he picked up Brownlow votes as well as club championship votes for his performance. Dawn has expressed her gratitude to me for inspiring her captain on several occasions since. I am so relieved it wasn't the Demons that Collingwood played that next week!

The dilemma, then, is whether to indulge in any serious imbibing *before* the schmoozing, or wait until *after*. I have also tried, on the strength of the previously described debacle, the latter approach. It was at the 2002 Women of Melbourne Luncheon. The pre-meal drinks were held in the downstairs foyer of the Park Hyatt. I grabbed a champagne (on this occasion just to keep my hands occupied, honestly) while keeping an eye out for the arrival of my guests as they made their grand entrances down the curved staircase. I planned to drink the bubbly, but not until *after* I had approached David Neitz for a photo with me. It was the first such luncheon at which I had seen Neita; on previous occasions I understand that he was studying for or sitting exams. So I was *very* keen to schmooze him, particularly as there were no cute little lambs (of course, I mean young fans) around, just mutton (rather, women) about my age and older. I figured I should just front up to Neita and get the nervy bit out of the way so I could relax and get on with enjoying the luncheon and the company of my girlfriends. Good plan?

Despite lacking a dose of Dutch courage, I managed to front up (jelly knees and all) to Neita, with Dawn at my side ever willing to take a picture (particularly as she wanted to test out her new digital camera). I even managed to make conversation and congratulate Neita on his excellent form so far for the season — I think I said something like, 'I expect to be congratulating you on winning the Coleman Medal at the B&F!' I sidled up to pose for the photo. Neita politely put his arm around me and I endeavoured to do the same to him. I was, by now, acutely aware of my nervousness and fumbled, accidentally slipping my arm *under* his coat as I put my arm around his waist (I prayed that he didn't notice — I didn't want him to think I was going the grope or anything!) Dawn clicked, but it was too late — I had already gone beetroot-red from the tips of my 14Cs right up to my widow's peak! I scurried away as quickly as I could and tried to keep a low profile for the rest of the function.

Once seated at our table, Dawn checked the photos she had already taken. (Oh, the wonders of modern technology!) I thought the photo of me was reasonable … for once (not that Dawn doesn't take a decent photograph, you understand, rather that I am not at all photogenic). Admittedly, my cheeks were a *very* deep shade of pink, but they often are, and I had certainly expected them to be after my faux pas. However, David Neitz had apparently blinked at precisely the wrong moment. (Groan!) His eyes were shut. Dawn cheerfully offered to take another photo (there was, after all, plenty of time!). But I was so embarrassed about my nervous fumble, and more embarrassed about the now blotchy colouration of my chest, neck and face (which, incidentally, didn't even begin to fade for about two hours, making me even more embarrassed, if at all possible!). *I just couldn't steel myself to approach Neita again that day.*

Dawn, appreciating my plight, refrained from attempting to drag me over for another shot with Neita. However, I almost came unstuck when, toward the end of the luncheon, Dawn showed me a great snap she had just taken of our friend, Sinead Wise, sitting on Russell Robertson's knee. I might have been red on the outside, but inside I was green! I had already schmoozed up to Robbo for a photo, but I could suddenly picture myself sitting on Neita's lap! Anyway, I had been chatting to Maree Royal, an old school friend (who also happens also to be the wife of MFC assistant coach, Brian Royal), when Dawn and Sinead found me, all excited as they were. Maree, on hearing about my spoiled photo, started calling Neita over to our table. 'Jelly knees' goes nowhere near describing my discomfort! Fortunately I was able to convince Maree that it wasn't the best time for a photo (my red blotches had re-emerged with a vengeance!).

How adolescent of us, you may well be thinking.

Schmoozing the effervescent Robbo at the 2002 Women of Melbourne Luncheon.

How can two so-called mature women indulge in such girlish, hero-worshipping, groupie type behaviour and still call themselves serious football supporters?

Well, as I understand it, that's what 'serious' football supporters do; attend functions where they try to meet their heroes, get their autographs, take photos with them, etcetera. We probably don't look that much like some of the fans that the general populace might identify as 'football groupies'. Then again, we don't actually consider ourselves 'groupies'.

The fact is we restrict our schmoozing up to the players to formal football club functions that the players are expected, even contracted by their club, to attend. I can honestly say on behalf of Dawn and myself that we wouldn't dream of approaching one of our own club's players (assuming we might actually see one) while out and about in the normal course of our daily lives — that would be infringing on his privacy! At club functions, however, the players in attendance are fair game. In fact, they are asked to attend such functions in order to attract a good turnout of club supporters!

Our partners and male acquaintances don't really seem to get it in respect of our interest in attending après football functions and schmoozing the players. Then again, they don't seem to be offended by it or object too strenuously to it, either. Mind you, we sometimes find it hard to understand the motivations of the many male fans that hang around the players at club functions. They often don't seem to realise when their conversation is boring the socks off the players. Of course (and the next line really *is* a joke), our aim in chatting to players is to bore the *pants* off them! (Ho, ho, ho!) That is just so never going to happen, right? Even if we might have entertained such a fantasy at some time in our lives. And conclusive proof that there isn't a chance in hell of anything untoward eventuating between ourselves and the AFL footballers we adore is that it's way too easy to get a leave pass from the hubbies to attend champagne football functions!

On a more serious note, Dawn has said that our pact to participate in the social side of our respective football clubs has rejuvenated her football life — it has even led to her attending more matches with friends rather than by herself.

(Sorry, Dawn … I think?) I believe that we are both now enjoying our football more than ever, and that attending matches and football-related social functions has become genuinely integrated into our everyday lives. Celebrating successes and milestones and commiserating losses is a normal part of life for people; as members of families, as members of staff teams at work, and as members of football clubs. Cheers to champagne football, and long may it reign! (Or should that be 'rain', as in rain bubbly?)

Penny ...

Captains of Football
A Social Worker's Perspective on Leadership

As you know, I've been attending the annual Women of Melbourne Luncheon since 1999. The Luncheon (funnily enough) is targeted at women. My girlfriends and I invariably enjoy a few drinks in moderation (that means I usually taxi home), and have a 'Cheers!' of a good time together, often kicking on for a bit later.

The luncheon is held at places like the Grand Hyatt or Park Hyatt in Melbourne, so it's not cheap (not that it's especially expensive — after all, even we social workers can afford it!). It's usually in the middle to latter part of the AFL Premiership Season, when the contenders for the final eight are starting to firm up. One of the main attractions is the plentiful supply of Melbourne football players who rock up. As my friend, Marg Downey, said at the 2002 function, 'Those boys are rather easy on the eye, you know.' (Oh yeah, nothing gets past me!)

At the 2002 luncheon, Pru Goward, the Federal Sex Discrimination Commissioner, was one of the guest speakers.

Pru spoke about the attributes common to successful women entrepreneurs that she had interviewed in the context of researching a book she had written. Pru's presentation, in which she gave a thorough description of her findings, could be described as very (and unsurprisingly) 'politically correct'. Crikey! I'm a social worker; I do the political correctness thing at work *every* day. A football club luncheon is no place for emphasising political correctness — after all, my girlfriends and I attend so we can actually ogle cute footballers!

Me and my girlfriends; MFC Women of Melbourne Luncheon 2002.

Needless to say, I was quite disappointed with Pru's talk. I felt that the attributes Pru identified sounded much the same as those evident among successful *male* entrepreneurs. So, if I can make comparisons between men and women, why couldn't

Pru? Why hadn't she tried to draw some links between her findings and the characteristics, for example, of successful *leaders* in team sports — especially footy, being the drawcard for the luncheon? And I was none too keen on the idea that maybe Pru assumed she was speaking to a room full of women who were successful in business. You don't have to be successful in the business world to be able to make a valuable financial contribution to your football club, *including MFC*, you know! Sure, a percentage of those in attendance were successful businesswomen, no doubt, but at my table alone there were two teachers, two bankers, a marketing consultant, an actor/comedian, and four social workers — no light bulb jokes, please! Some of us could be described as *leaders*, or at least fulfilling some leadership functions, within our respective organisations despite that we are not 'successful businesswomen'.

Leadership is a subject of particular interest to me. The social work profession has a long history of undertaking supervision as the major vehicle for providing four key functions: enhancing practice knowledge (education or professional development); ensuring that the specific policies, procedures and practice standards of the employing organisation are known and adhered to by the staff (accountability); maintaining worker morale (support); and liaising between base grade staff and senior management (mediation).

Responsibility for provision of the supervisory functions is not always vested exclusively in the supervisor. It is not at all unusual for the education function, in particular, but also the support function, to be spread across a range of individuals, methods and forums. The choice of delivery mode for the various functions varies according to the mix of practice skills, experience, maturity, and individual needs of the social workers in the team being supervised; the supervisory skills, experience and leadership style of the supervisor or team leader; and the policies, priorities and expectations (sometimes even the budget) of the senior managers of the employing agency in regard to supervision.

You probably weren't expecting a thesis on social work supervision right now (neither was I!). But when I think about it, supervisory functions and leadership in social work practice provide a useful framework for analysing the various coaching and leadership functions in football. (Really!)

In football clubs, just as in social work agencies, responsibility for the various functions may be vested in a number of individuals and delivered via a range of methods. For example, the senior coach has overall responsibility for the management of the team and its players, and for ensuring that each player understands and abides by the club's values, and endeavours to implement the strategies developed for the team to the best of his abilities (accountability). However, assistant and specialist coaches share the training load in relation to improving the fitness and specific skills of individual players (education/development function); the coach, assistant coaching and training staff, the captain, the team's leadership group and senior players all share the task of motivating and sustaining player morale (support function); and the captain, supported by his vice-captains and other senior players, liaises and negotiates between the players and coaching staff and/or club management, as necessary (mediation). Individual players may also have personal mentors, such as their manager, father, or other hero outside the club structure, who assists them by providing ongoing support and career guidance.

If it all sounds complex, that's because it is. The situation in football seems much simpler, however, when the players are on the ground with a match in progress. Okay, players may be sent messages from the coach via a runner during the course of the match (education and/or accountability). A player may even be dragged from the ground to ensure that a message is heard directly from the coach over the phone (definitely accountability on some occasions, for example, when a player has just given away a 50-metre penalty that results in an opposition goal!). But the players are essentially out there by themselves once the umpire blows his whistle and bounces the oval ball. This is where the team captain takes on a much more significant role in leading his team-mates, and where his leadership style and abilities come under particular scrutiny — by the coaching staff, club officials, supporters and fans ... and the media. It is the captain's on-field performance that can make a significant difference in a tight encounter, or can ensure that his team shellacs a weaker opposition rather than merely winning the match by a few points.

Selecting the captain is clearly an important decision not to be taken lightly, and is not necessarily a straightforward one. Just as in social work, this decision must take into account the current and future needs of the team, and the characteristics and maturity of the individual players in the team, as well as the particular strengths and style of the individual leader.

And make no mistake, choosing an individual to take on

additional, designated responsibility for the management and morale of his peers is difficult — probably a lot more difficult than choosing a coach from the wider football community to come into a club. A coach appointed from outside has to *establish new* relationships with all the players, unless he happens to have coached one or some of them previously at another club. And it is likely that he will already have credibility in the role of coach or assistant coach from his previous experience. But a newly appointed captain has *existing* relationships with *all* his team-mates, and has to *change* the nature of those relationships somewhat. He may also have to deal with one or more peers, who are also good friends, and who believe they have as much credibility or potential to fulfil the captain's role as he does. The only thing simpler in football, and I mean AFL, regarding the transition from peer to captain compared with being appointed to supervisor in social work, is that there aren't any gender issues. Regardless of how well cooked or apparently underdone on his appointment, the captain is always going to be a bloke, and so are all the other players!

Now that the reader is all primed up with the relevant theoretical framework ('according to Penny', anyway), at last (and I'm sure you're very relieved to know this!) *it's time to explore the real world of on-field football leadership*. Often it appears that the player with the best football skills in the team is the one who gets to be captain, right?

Take Hawthorn, for example. Shane Crawford, the 1999 Brownlow Medallist, is their captain. He is a superb player and clearly an inspiration to his team-mates — a dashing, flamboyant midfielder who is a high possession-getter with pace, endurance, great delivery and finishing, and plenty of courage. Not only that, but he consistently puts in throughout a match, particularly at times when the game is there to be won, week in and week out. Now, try to name the second best player at Hawthorn. Daniel Chick was pretty good (though now he plays for the West Coast Eagles), and Angelo Lekkas, Nathan Thompson and Nick Holland are all okay. But really, Crawford seems to me to be head and shoulders (metaphorically speaking, that is) above the rest of the players at that club. And let's face it, it must be pretty hard to look classy and stand out from the pack when you and your team-mates are dressed in poo colors!

Collingwood's captain, Nathan Buckley, has been a consistently outstanding player since he set boot on a footy field. He must be one of the most accurate kicks in the game, and has won the Collingwood Best and Fairest award on a record five occasions. There are certainly some other solid performers in the team, like Scott Burns, and a bunch of other maturing players who are very skilled and improving in or consolidating their consistency — including Paul Licuria, Anthony Rocca and Tarkyn Lockyer.

But Buckley really stands up when the team needs him. Who could forget the 2002 Grand Final? — Dawn certainly won't in a hurry! Buckley's performance was inspirational. The match was a truly epic encounter and, unfortunately for Collingwood, they didn't win the flag. But it wasn't for lack of effort on the captain's part, which was duly noticed by those who awarded the Norm Smith Medal for the best player on the ground that day.

The Western Bulldogs captain, Chris Grant, is another leader who for many years has been a standout class player in his team. Grant's enduring significance to his team and Club's performance is best highlighted by the shattering impact of his season-ending injury in 2003. Again, there are other excellent and consistent performers in the team, like Scott West, Brad Johnson, Rohan Smith, Luke Darcy and Nathan Brown. However, Grant's uncanny ability to do the seemingly impossible, enabling his team to get up and win crucial matches against the odds, is what sets him apart from his team-mates. Well, that and his loyal response to a young fan who sent in his pocket money (I think it was the princely sum of twenty cents) in a generous gesture to stop Grant being lured by a big-money contract to another club at a time when the Bulldogs almost went under financially. Talk about playing football for the love of the game! What passion! It couldn't possibly get any more sentimental than that.

The downside of the captain needing to be an elite foot-baller, however, is the expectation that he will *always* perform at that level. This can place enormous external pressure on the individual (as if he hasn't already set his own lofty standards to live up to). On the one hand, you could argue that the captain is selected on the basis that he can handle this additional pressure, and that's fair enough. But it can appear a bit rough to diehard supporters when the coach 'has a word' to an ageing captain (that is, one in his thirties). For example, the decision that was apparently made *for* Matthew Knights, as opposed to being made *by* Matthew Knights, to step down as captain of Richmond for season 2001 didn't seem to go down real well with Tigers fans. Such action can seem particularly harsh if the captain is struggling to overcome niggling injuries and missing training sessions, let alone matches. However, it's equally valid to argue that it is impossible for a player to be an effective *on*-field leader if he's hardly ever *on* the field during match time.

Another example of this is when, at the end of season 1997, Neale Daniher, the then newly appointed senior coach of Melbourne, suggested to Garry Lyon that he should step down from the captaincy so Todd Viney could take up the post. Lyon was a true blue (and red, of course) Demon, with a legion of supporters. He was as mentally tough and determined as any captain in the AFL, but his body was stubbornly refusing to measure up, with a persistent back injury preventing him from training and playing regularly.

It is fair to say that, in appointing a captain, the coaching staff and club officials expect that player to be able to do the extra one-per-centers that can turn a match, and do them consistently.

Michael Voss, captain of the Brisbane Lions and 1996 co-Brownlow Medallist, is a skipper who I'd definitely put in that category. In fact, I find it hard to argue that he is not the best captain in the AFL at the present time. Voss can appear to be having a quiet day (relative to his standards), then bob up with a crucial play that results in the winning goal in the dying minutes of a match. In fact, in his team there are at least half a dozen blokes who can do that — like Simon Black (2002 Brownlow Medallist), Jason Akermanis (2001 Brownlow Medallist), Chris Johnson, Chris Scott, Brad Scott, Shaun Hart and Daniel Bradshaw. It was, as it turned out, a highly skilled play by Jason Akermanis to win the ball and kick a difficult goal late in the final quarter that won the 2002 Premiership for the Lions.

So why isn't Jason Akermanis captain of the Brisbane Lions? Well, there is more to being a captain than being an elite player, or even *the* superstar of the team. The 'leading by example' element of being an AFL captain extends to more than just the skill level and quality of the footballer's performances. The captain's non-playing performance is equally important; it can either strengthen or undermine his playing role. The things he says in interviews with the media, the way he conducts himself in his private life, the example he sets away from the spotlight of the football arena, and the congruence between the player's demeanour on and off the field, all count.

Getting back to Jason Akermanis for a moment. He is a flamboyant player, just like Shane Crawford. He has the capacity to play consistently and of a high standard, like Nathan Buckley. And he has demonstrated an ability to bob up with an inspirational play at the crucial moment to win an important match, just like his own captain, Michael Voss. Yet, his flamboyance on the field often spills over into spontaneous and, one could say, ill-considered comments on controversial, or potentially controversial, matters that are played up by the media.

This is something that a club could not, and should not, tolerate in its captain. Such behaviour may be acceptable in another player, providing some colour and character to the team. Indeed, there is room for all sorts of roles to be filled in a team, and there is always a natural 'clown' or 'comedian' in a group. For example, the not quite politically correct Russell 'Robbo' Robertson of the Melbourne Demons is as cheeky and unpredictable off the field as he is on it. However, there is a good reason why we don't see Michael Voss shooting from the hip on various matters. As captain he is a nominated representative of his club and must take all the potential ramifications of any comments he makes into account, rather than merely represent his own personal views.

Those selecting the captain would want to choose someone on whom they could *rely* to 'say the right thing'. How could the Lions go wrong with such a clean-cut, clean living, all round good guy and family man like Michael Voss?

But on second thoughts, I think some of Shane Crawford's antics have probably pushed the envelope with the coaching staff and committee of the Hawthorn Football Club at various times. What about the time he dacked someone on live television, or when he took off his own shorts at the end of a match, or his acting role in *The House of Bulger*?

I hold firmly to my position that the captain's general *off*-field behaviour, as distinguished from any comments he might make to or in the media, is also critical in reinforcing his credibility as an *on*-field leader.

Perhaps the most glaring example is that of Wayne Carey. This was undoubtedly the biggest story of the 2002 pre-season. It was ridiculously, embarrassingly, even nauseatingly, big. In short, it was *too* big. The unprecedented media fascination with the Carey thing is a story in itself. After all, we are talking about a real, Australian football player and not some pseudonym of a Hollywood movie star! But the story does need to be viewed in the context of Carey, at the age of 21 in 1993, being the youngest VFL/AFL captain ever appointed. Carey was a superstar of the game — an inspirational, possession getting, goal kicking and match winning team player for the Kangaroos. Many, especially Kangaroos supporters, felt he was the heart and soul of his team. It was blasphemous, even for supporters of other clubs, to entertain the idea of Carey ever playing with another AFL club. But early in 2002 it was revealed that he had been having an affair with the wife of his vice-captain and good mate, Anthony Stevens. (Whoops!)

The damage done to the relationship between Carey and Stevens, and between Carey and the other senior players at the Kangaroos, was irreparable. Carey was obliged to step down from his captaincy and leave the Kangaroos. The trust and friendship of his mates and team-mates had been betrayed. As the captain, it would be expected (under normal circumstances) that Carey would provide support to his team-mates in a time of crisis and distress. But how could he when *he* was a primary source of that distress? Many questions come to mind: Was Carey appointed to the captaincy at too young an age — that is, was he undercooked? Is there a certain level of personal maturity and life experience that should be attained before a player is given the privilege and responsibility of the captain's mantle? Did appointment to captain make this player arrogant, or exacerbate such a pre-existing attitude in him?

Whatever, Carey clearly made a big mistake. A mistake that will cloud people's perceptions of his character for the rest of his career. A mistake that should make all AFL clubs even more carefully consider their criteria and processes for selecting and supporting captains in the future.

The real story of courage and leadership to emerge from the Carey saga involves, almost incredibly, the most wronged party in the whole sorry mess — Anthony Stevens — who was betrayed by both his wife and one of his best mates. Stevens and good friend and fellow senior team-mate, another former best mate of Carey, Glenn Archer, were selected as the new captain and vice-captain, respectively, of the Kangaroos. This pair demonstrated great courage, dignity and leadership to maintain their team's morale, defying the critics and spearheading their team's run into the 2002 finals series.

Courage is certainly a key characteristic common to on-field leaders in the AFL. James Hird's story is nothing short of amazing. In 2002 he suffered serious cranio-facial injuries on colliding with the knee of one of his own team-mates, Mark McVeigh, in a marking contest during Essendon's Round 6 match against Fremantle in Perth. Hird underwent major surgery and, incredibly, resumed his place at the Bombers' helm early in the second half of the season (Round 14, to be precise). He subsequently led his team into yet another finals series. I'm sure there are many players who would have retired from football altogether after sustaining such injuries, but not Hird. Love him or hate him (and I'd like to hate him because I'm not yet ready to forgive him for so inspirationally leading the team that beat mine in our Grand Final appearance in 2000!), even I have to acknowledge that Hird has bucketloads of courage and determination. He has an indomitable strength, both of body and of mind.

Being supportive to the other players is something that can be learned and improved with practice. The most frequent displays of support occur after a goal is kicked. There may be high fives all round, a few ruffles of the hair, lots of pats on the butt, or even a bearhug among the players (that's when I'd *most* like to put myself in a footballer's boots). But one of the first to congratulate is almost invariably the captain. Unless it's the captain who kicked the goal, of course, in which case he will generally zoom up to the team-mate who delivered the ball to him first, and then to any other players who were instrumental in the play, and give a pat, ruffle, high five, accompanied by a few words of encouragement. I don't lip read very well, but I imagine they say macho, blokesy sorts of things like, 'Onya Ooze!' or 'Bloody bewdy Browny!' or 'Stick it right up 'em!' or 'Great f***in' stuff!' or 'Where's *my* f***in' hug, you big oaf?' — maybe not the last one (that's probably what I'd say).

Similarly, you will sometimes see the captain make the effort to run to a player, particularly a younger, less experienced team-mate, who causes a turnover that results in an opposition goal. Such a goal could be the difference between winning and losing a tight match. But a show of support by the captain is obviously good for the morale and self-confidence of the player concerned; it demonstrates that the team leader has faith in that player, and helps him refocus on what he *can* do to help his team win rather than on his mistake. In this way, the captain also subtly (do footballers have that in their repertoire?) reminds the other members of his team that no player deliberately sets out to make mistakes, and that it could have been any one of *them*.

Little wonder, methinks, that Matthew Richardson, one of the stars of Richmond, was not appointed to the captaincy at his club for 2002. Who will ever forget that Friday night match (actually, I can't quite recall which Round it was!)

during the season when big Richo spat the dummy and gave young David Rodan a spray for missing a goal from about a metre out and right in front? Richo then dropped his shoulders and appeared to give up when, a few minutes later, Rodan delivered the ball poorly to him. I think Richo deserved the criticism his behaviour attracted on that occasion. Like, hello! You don't have to be a social worker to appreciate that behaviour like that is no way to support and nurture the confidence of younger team-mates.

To Richardson's credit, during the rest of 2002 he appeared to be putting his best foot forward, trying very hard to improve his supportiveness and responsiveness to other players, and to maintain his own positive attitude when things were not going his way. I thought he did a great job of captaining the Tigers in that exhibition match against the Bombers in London after the 2002 Grand Final. (Any win over the Bombers is to be applauded, and just focusing on the match and ignoring all the drunken flashers and streakers in the crowd would have been an achievement!)

Team-mates also look to their captain for support in a physical sense when they come under direct flak from opposition players. It's a bonus if the captain happens to be big and burly, especially one whose position is on the ball, like the Port Power ruckman, Matthew Primus. A 'Johnny-on-the-spot' captain can obviously lend valuable support to his team-mates whenever they are subject to unwanted physical attention. I've often seen the likes of Primus and Ben Graham, Geelong's former captain, chest up to opposition players who are picking on their smaller team-mates, or simply put their big bodies between their team-mate and the aggressors. And I've seen David Neitz run from one end of the ground to the other to defend a team-mate.

It cuts the other way too. I'm sure it's most helpful for a player to have his big burly captain holding onto his jumper, barking out a few instructions to settle him down when things are getting a bit heated. After all, no good can come from doing something impulsive that may result in an audience at the tribunal. Further, it is one of the captain's responsibilities to help maintain appropriate calm and focus (and what an enviable job that must be, roughing it amongst all the litres of testosterone and adrenalin pumping around those sweaty male bodies! Ouch!)

What the smaller captains may lack in physical size, they make up for in other qualities and skills; especially verbal skills — niggling and the odd spray being the main offensive weapons. Remember Tony Shaw, Collingwood's 1990 Premiership captain — he may not have been tall but he certainly lacked for nothing in the perseverance and verbal departments!

A corollary of the supportive or nurturing role of the captain is his humility. The quality captains never seem to talk up their own performances, and never put too many 'I's in their responses to questions from members of the media. They always refer to the good performances of their team-mates, and play down their own role in their team's success.

Take David Neitz again (oh, yes please!). He invariably talks about his team-mates rather than himself. Even when asked about his sensational seven-goal effort in Round 14 of 2002 in Brisbane, which helped Melbourne beat the Brisbane Lions (the eventual back-to-back Premiers), Neita was praising 'the boys' on their efforts. He constantly deflected personal praise onto the great performances of other players in ensuring that the ball was effectively delivered to him, saying he was 'fortunate' to be able to finish off their great plays. Fortunate! He was *the* in form full-forward of the competition for most of the season. His nine goals in Round 15 against Carlton was the biggest goal haul by *any* player in 2002!

The quality captains also take it upon themselves to shoulder much of the responsibility for their team's losses, always saying 'we' and often pointing to themselves as having been 'unable to lift', or having been outplayed by their direct opponent. It's really the opposite quality to arrogance in a footballer, in my opinion. The good captains also seem to take criticism quite well; they take it on the chin, present as being philosophical, and try to draw out the positives by identifying their team's and their own challenges for the next match or season. I know it's very clichéd in football parlance now, but the old 'just taking one match at a time' line is a good example of the captain (or coach) not getting ahead of himself.

To summarise, the characteristics and qualities required of an AFL captain appear to include: excellent football skills and the ability to maintain consistent and elite playing form and fitness; a willingness and capacity to lead by example and to inspire their team-mates through their own courageous play, enthusiasm and passion for the game, strong work ethic, untiring contributions and second efforts; the ability to handle pressure, both physically and mentally; congruence in their on-field and off-field behaviour, including that they manage any flamboyance such that they avoid controversy and do not bring their own, nor their club's, reputation into disrepute; the capacity to be supportive through words and actions, and to encourage positive behaviours and discourage negative behaviours in their team-mates; and to be humble, generous in praise of their team-mates, and able to turn poor performances and criticism into motivating challenges.

Crikey! And I used to think that was such a good description of David Neitz.

I'm sure I heard Bruce McAvaney introduce Neita as 'a true superstar of the game' one night on *Talking Footy* at the end of the 2002 premiership season. Indeed, David Neitz has demonstrated an ability to play in key positions at both ends of the field, though he has most certainly cemented himself as the permanent full-forward of MFC having clearly won the 2002 Coleman Medal, awarded to the leading goal kicker in the home-and-away season. In 2002, he also won two MFC awards: one for the club's best and fairest player and another for inspirational performance. He was also named an All-Australian for the second time in his career.

I had long been of the opinion that Neitz was a quality ingredient for a successful Premiership recipe, though clearly not everyone was as convinced as I of his credentials for the MFC captaincy on his appointment in season 2000. (Did they know something I didn't?) It seemed to me that Neitz had the ability to handle pressure, both physically and psychologically. Otherwise he would surely have crumbled under the criticisms and questions abounding at the time of his appointment. Instead, he responded like any true champion by putting runs on the board — particularly during season 2002.

Neita's capacity to handle pressure has again been seriously tested during the first half of season 2003. Neitz has found himself the target of concerted opposition defence on the field, just like Shane Woewodin (how I miss him!) did after his stellar Brownlow Medal-winning season of 2000. Some cracks seem to have appeared in Neita's offensive arsenal as a result of the double and triple teaming he now endures every time the ball comes his way. His responses have at times been uncharacteristically undisciplined; most notably in aggressive incidents against the Fremantle Dockers during Round 9 and the Adelaide Crows during Round 12. These incidents were not sufficiently outlandish to result in Neitz fronting the AFL tribunal but they did result in inopportune free kicks to the opposition and they weren't pretty, either.

The Demons won two of their first three matches of 2003. A third victory came in Round 7, but no further points were added to their Premiership tally up to the mid-season break following Round 12. Neitz was described in the media as struggling for form, frustrated and angry. Mike Sheahan wrote, 'The worse Melbourne has performed, the more frustrated the skipper has become ... an accident waiting to happen.'[8]

Since the apparently inevitable incident (if you believe Sheahan, that is) at Crown Casino at around 3.00 a.m. on Tuesday, 17 June 2003, I'm not as confident as I was previously about the quality of Neita's leadership capabilities. Neitz was endeavouring to catch a taxi home, apparently inebriated after a social evening with his team-mates that was designed to put their disastrous first half of the season behind them. Neitz was refused a ride by two cab drivers, then a third insisted on a deposit first. Neita apparently lost his cool and was physically restrained by several security officers until police arrived and escorted him to his girlfriend's home.

> *I have always admired the*
> *'Coming through! Man with a*
> *skinful of testosterone and desperate*
> *to get his hands on the footy!'*
> *style of play that so characterises*
> *David Neitz on the football field.*

But it is important to be able to maintain self-control and to draw an appropriate line in the social setting. 'Coming through! Man with a skinful of booze and desperate to catch a cab and go home!' is not a good look for an AFL captain off the football field, especially not for the captain of *my* team.

The media subsequently reported that this was not the first off-field incident in which my club's skipper had been involved — there had apparently been two incidents as recently as 1999, the year before he commenced his captaincy. I for one had not heard about any prior 'incidents' involving Neita, and I was as shocked and disappointed as anyone to hear about them — well, maybe a little more so. To say I was shattered would not be an understatement.

Prior to the June 2003 incident, I was unswerving in my belief that David Neitz was the complete package as far as an AFL captain was concerned — a champion and a gentleman. (I can be a real sycophant when I like someone.) He always seemed so confident, in control, affable and relaxed to me. I assure you that it would take more than a few alcohol-fuelled scuffles with Crown Casino bouncers before I contemplated removing my favourite player's badge from my Demon jumper. But heroes are human after all, and my blind faith in Neita's ability to lead my team to football's Holy Grail — the elusive Premiership Cup — in the not too distant future has been shaken. I now know that there are chinks in his leadership repertoire.

Neita and me on a good night at Crown.

Maybe I'm over-reacting. But if, as a devoted Demons supporter and David Neitz fan, I am feeling somewhat battered and bruised by the recent revelations about his involvement in some unsavoury off-field behaviour, imagine how hard he will have to work to regain the respect and confidence of the players he is directly responsible for leading on-field. It may be my social work perspective but I am under no illusions that it will be easy for Neita to work through this leadership crisis. I sincerely hope that Neitz isn't either. I guess we will just have to wait and see how he responds. Oh, what a fun topic of conversation that will be when I'm schmoozing up to him at the next Women of Melbourne Luncheon!

As a social worker I would not presume to give anyone advice — a person must be able to draw their own conclusions from the information available to them before making a genuine commitment to change their behaviour. But as a final word on the always complex and sometimes also fraught subject of leadership in relation to the performances of AFL captains, I will say that one couldn't possibly go wrong with Michael Voss as a role model. Oh, and one more thing. If some smart-arse tries to find so much as a skerrick of dust let alone a pinch of dirt on Vossy, I promise I'll sue them for intentional and malicious damage to the dream of a perfect AFL captain. I mean it!

Football, Dad and Me

As long as I can remember — and it's a pretty long time — I have loved sport. I must qualify that and explain that I love *watching* sport. When I was younger, I quite liked playing sport, but I was never very good. It wasn't from lack of effort (well, at the beginning anyway), but when it came to ball sports, I was lost. I had no idea where the ball was most of the time. Netball was okay. The ball was so big that even I knew where it was, but anything smaller than that was a disaster. (I'll never know why they call it softball — I've been hit in the face by one several times and I can tell you that it's not at all soft!)

Not to make excuses, but my lack of coordination, which was written off as clumsiness when I was young, is actually the result of my lack of depth perception! Unfortunately I was seventeen before this was correctly diagnosed, and by this time the damage was done. The spirit which had once been willing was now gone and the only games I played were in my dreams. There I was, watching Wimbledon and desperately

Dawn, full of enthusiasm, aged two.

dreaming of being Margaret Court, and sitting in for every session of the Olympics and boldly telling my mother that I was going to be an athlete when I grew up — I'll never know how she kept a straight face with that one! The important thing was that I watched sport.

I blame my father for my budding couch potato tendencies! Dad will admit that he could be bribed to do almost anything if it meant an uninterrupted afternoon watching 'the game' on TV. I recall many a Saturday when Mum and I headed off to the shops for some girl bonding and retail therapy, leaving Dad with the vacuum, ironing board or the brasses. 'The game' Dad was (and still is) especially fond of is rugby — the game they play in heaven you know! Rugby is particularly close to home as he was a fine amateur grade player in his own right and I have clear memories of being taken to see him play — of the oranges at half time and the really nasty language, but that's another story.

The other most watched game and one with which I had a greater allegiance in my younger years was football!

I am of course referring to soccer, to which I was addicted at a very early age. When it came to team allegiance, I can't remember making the decision myself, so I have a fair idea I was indoctrinated in the cradle. My father is a Manchester United fan and so was I. It was that simple! They won the 1968 European Cup — this was a golden era for United and I revelled in it. I remember my mother coming up and getting me out of bed (quietly so my little brother wasn't disturbed) so that I could watch the match. The memories of that epic final will live with me forever!

Things could have continued in this manner indefinitely but my father's restless and ambitious nature intervened. We could have gone anywhere — the Amazon region and Canada were both mentioned at different stages — but the serious contenders for our new home were South Africa and Australia. Looking back, I realise that South Africa must have been a very real option. I recall being sick as an eight-year-old and Dad getting me some books from the library. In retrospect, *The History of the Springbok Rugby Team* and a South African travel guide probably weren't the books I'd have chosen for a convalescing eight-year-old, but it gives you an idea of his thought processes at the time.

For better or worse, however, Australia became our chosen destination and we arrived in this glorious country in July 1971. Our earliest destination was Wollongong — keep the jokes to yourselves please! — which was our home for a year. My interest in football waned somewhat during that year; we weren't there long enough to take more than a cursory interest in the Rugby League, although I do admit to a passing interest in St George. I suspect this had more to do with my Anglophile nature than any real interest in the sport or the club. It was a year in which we marked time until we moved south to Australia's home of sport — Melbourne.

The year was 1972 and I arrived in Melbourne with my family in September. The timing was quite impeccable as it coincided with the commencement of the finals series — although I must confess that I remained largely immune to the significance of the event. Naturally, I had heard of Aussie Rules. I'd been told of this strange game played by the natives of the Southern states, but I hadn't seen much of it. Still, it was clear to me that it was necessary to support a team or I'd be left out — a truly disastrous thought for a pre-teenager!

The problem was *which team to adopt?*

My father had done his homework and was determined to get off to a good start with his chosen team, while my brother and I were less sure and swithered over the decision. 'What about St Kilda?' I said, thinking that a continuation of the ecclesiastical theme may be a good omen.

'How about Essendon?' asked Neale, for no apparent reason, although one suspects that the nickname of the Bombers may have impressed him.

'Forget them,' said Dad, with all the wisdom of one who

has read an edition or two of the *Herald*, 'there're only two teams worth bothering with.' We waited with bated breath as he continued, 'No, if you're serious about football, you've got to follow Carlton or Collingwood.' I'm sure it was purely co-incidental that these teams then occupied the top two positions. No, there it was, the word of the master — but there was more.

'Well,' I said, 'who are you going for, Dad?' I didn't know then the importance of his next words …

> but in that moment I took the first bold
> steps toward my obsession.

'Carlton,' he replied, with all the confidence of one whose team were favourites for the Premiership, 'I reckon I'll support the Blues!'

I swear that I don't know what happened next! I'd always been a dutiful daughter, had done what I was told and fol-lowed the lead of my parents in all things (hadn't I followed Manchester United from the cradle?), but somewhere inside me there was clearly a rebellious spark that made me respond, 'Well if you're going for Carlton, I'll go for Collingwood. That should make things more interesting!' More interesting! If I had only known then of the years of frustration, peppered with triumph, that those words were going to cause me! Dad smiled indulgently at me in much the same way that he did years later when, in my next burst of rebellion as a radical university student, I told him I was voting Labor. And so the battle begun!

I recall the early games that I went to with my father and

brother at the MCG — actually, what I remember most is driving around the St Kilda Junction three times as we desperately tried to work out how to get up Punt Rd. As the eldest I was designated navigator. So, armed with a five year old Melways and absolutely no local knowledge, I proceeded to get hopelessly lost in the building site which is now the Junction. On the third circumnavigation, tired of having my father call me things that no thirteen-year-old should hear and desperate to get to the game before the first siren — any siren, at that point — I closed my eyes and pointed wildly, saying 'turn here!' As luck would have it I was right. My reputation was saved, we saw the opening bounce, I never forgot how to get to Punt Road again, and I decided there and then that public transport looked like a great way to get to the football! This was a thought that was only enhanced when, instead of enjoying a post game review as we trundled home again, my brother, father and I spent three quarters of an hour trying to find the bloody car in the bloody car park! Do you have any idea how many green Valiants were around in 1973? Well, they were all at the MCG that day! Ready to call the police, convinced that our car had been stolen (and after another burst of unattractive language — I'm so ashamed of myself) we finally found the car, parked one row back from where we were sure we had left it!

Throughout much of the seventies I was a supporter in name only. I knew of a few players (Billy Picken and Rene Kink were two of my early favourites) but my interest was largely a cursory one. I remember going to a couple of games with Dad but none of them involved Collingwood so they are only vague memories.

Finally, in 1980, Dad took me to see Collingwood for the first time. We went to VFL Park at Waverley which was only half an hour from home. The decision was made at the last minute, after I'd nagged for a couple of hours. Dad put on a great show of reluctance which fooled nobody, before finally agreeing and telling me to hurry up because he wasn't going to wait around! On this occasion we saw Collingwood take on St Kilda. This match is well known as the occasion that saw a St Kilda player take a kick at a stray dog that had wandered onto the pitch. Animal lovers need not worry, the dog was unhurt — St Kilda couldn't get a kick to save themselves that day! Oh, the wit! And it was comments such as that one which made the day so unforgettable for my father. It will surprise no-one who knows me, but I am fairly vocal about things. Get me to the football, with the adrenaline running rampant and I am even worse! Knowing this, Dad thought he could neutralise my impact by sitting me in the middle of a group of St Kilda supporters. His reasoning was that this would frighten me into keeping my mouth shut! How wrong he was! I was in fine form this day and thoroughly enjoying Collingwood's domination of the match. My comments were probably a little unfair and clearly upset the Saints supporter in front of me. As I made a witticism (my words!) about the dog incident, the frustrated supporter, having taken as much as a man could, swung round to confront his tormentor! The problem was, as I was recovering from a cold and have quite a deep voice at the best of times, he had assumed that I was a male. When he discovered I wasn't you could see chivalry battling with anger. In the end, he struck my dad! Just a glancing blow/shove and a suggestion he keep me under

better control! The only thing damaged was Dad's ego —
although father-daughter relations were severely strained. It
took several nights of making coffee and washing dishes
before he got over it and Dad never deliberately sat with the
opposition supporters again!

Despite this, Dad did take me to the football again. It was
Easter Monday, 1981, and Mum wanted us out of the house
so that she could make my twenty-first birthday cake. So off
we went to the football! On this day VFL Park recorded its
biggest ever football crowd as Collingwood took on the
Hawks. I remember sitting on the step in the aisle in complete
breach of all safety regulations, and Leigh Matthews carving
Collingwood up as he booted eight goals (who would have
thought that only nine years later he was to become the hero
of Victoria Park?).

And then there was the car park. The problems of the
Waverley car park have become legendary and this day was
the most pressing example. It took us over an hour to get out!
And these were the days before mobile phones so there was
no calling home to let Mum know that we were all right. We
finally got home at about 7.30 p.m. — cold, hungry, tired and
really cheesed off at the result. I've never been a good loser!

After that, when it came to footy, Dad and I went our sep-
arate ways. I think he thought I'd subjected him to enough
trauma by then. I found other football-loving friends and
finally, in the nineties, became a regular attendee at
Collingwood games. Dad moved interstate to Adelaide where
his interest in the game waxed and waned.

My favourite Crows supporter.

Some of Dad's earlier interest returned in 1992 with the advent of the Adelaide Crows. He even committed the unthinkable sin of changing his allegiance from Carlton to Adelaide! As you can imagine I had much to endure during Adelaide's triumphs in 1997 and 1998, particularly given Collingwood's lowly status at that time! I know he was pleased — and the Crows were very impressive — but beginning every phone conversation with 'we're the pride of South Australia' was just a bit much for me!

In 1999, while researching this book, Penny and I decided that we should jointly experience the delights of an interstate football jaunt. I, of course, was an old hat at it (I'd been twice before!) but Penny was a novice. Our not-so-fanatical friend,

Keri, decided that she'd enjoy the trip so the three of us made plans.

At my request we decided to go to Adelaide to see Collingwood take on the Crows at Football Park. I could enjoy the football and see my Dad at the same time — luckily the others agreed.

Dad bravely decided to join us and subsequently found himself at Football Park with three thoroughly over-excited females — okay, only Penny and I were over-excited but Keri was on the way! He was quite comfortable at the pre-match Collingwood dinner, enjoying his roast and the speech made by Magpie legend (and South Australian) Murray Weideman. We checked our match tickets and noticed that we were close to the front. 'Excellent,' thought Penny and I. 'I hope I don't get hit by the ball,' thought Keri. 'I hope no one recognises me,' thought Dad. Dad's unease turned to horror when we discovered where our seats were. He'd expected to be sur-rounded by Collingwood supporters but not to end up in the middle of the Collingwood cheer squad!

When we first arrived, the front row was empty as the cheer squad battled with the banner. When they returned the fun began! They unzipped a huge canvas bag and a seemingly endless number of paddys emerged.

For the uninitiated, a paddy is the pompom on a stick you see being shaken up and down with enthusiasm, as opposed to the 'flogger', which is the bloody big pompom that hangs over the fence. These are banned at Football Park — spoil-sports! Anyway, I digress.

Penny and I accepted our paddys with glee; this was heaven for a couple of diehards like us! Keri demurred saying they were too heavy for her, and Dad, well, he just looked horrified! I had to act quickly.

'He barracks for Adelaide!' I blurted. Whoops! Not a good move! Smiles turned to frowns and muttering started. 'But he used to barrack for Carlton …' I blundered on.

Oh no! Was this worse? No, on the contrary, the smiles returned and the muttering ceased. Even so, Dad quailed as a fearsome-looking gentleman dressed in a Magpies guernsey lunged — I mean leaned — toward him holding out his hand.

'Well, even the Crows are better than bloody Carlton. Have a good night!' With that he shook Dad's hand and turned back toward the pitch. Phew, got out of that one. Just in case I suggested to Dad that he restrain himself if Adelaide got on top — the thought of someone barracking for the Crows from the middle of the Collingwood cheer squad was too much to contemplate. I don't think he was really comfortable at all through the match. As Penny and I shook our paddys and chanted with enthusiasm, Dad fidgeted, muttering something about seeing us in the bar.

Sadly for me, the Crows recovered after Collingwood led all night in a nail-biting match. An extremely dubious umpiring decision in the last seconds of the match cost us a kick at goal. Dad refrained from saying anything that may have upset the already angry and disappointed Collingwood army, and some time later, when he was well away from anyone that might hear him, he actually conceded that we were robbed!

I'm pleased to say that Dad did recover from his early scare and was actually heard to comment on the professionalism and excellent behaviour of the Collingwood crowd. He even agreed to escort his girls to the post-match function where he sat by paternally while Penny and I chased autographs and photos of my vanquished heroes.

All the same, Dad was obviously shaken by his experience. He passed on my suggestion that we go to the 2001 Collingwood versus Port Adelaide Power game, citing health problems. (Can you imagine, I went over to Adelaide that weekend and spent match night listening to it on the radio about ten kilometres from Feral — I mean Football — Park!)

You could really feel sorry for my dad for what I've put him through. Fear not, however, because in 2002 Dad got his revenge on me, and in my mind at least, we're even now!

Early in the year, I advised Dad that as I had enough FlyBuy points, it was a good time for me to visit and make sure he was okay.

'Terrific!' said Dad. 'When are you coming?'

I grabbed the footy fixture and noted the highlighted dates of Collingwood's two Adelaide games. 'Well, Dad, I thought I might come over for one of the matches, either May or July. Now you don't have to come ...' I hurried on, remembering our past experiences. To my surprise, Dad was remarkably relaxed about the whole thing.

'Why don't you make it May?' he said. 'Come over for the Port game and I'll see if I can get the corporate box from work.'

Beauty, how civilised is this? Collingwood away (and we beat them there last year), get to see Dad and schmooze in a corporate box. What more could a girl want? I hastily agreed and booked my seat as soon as possible.

Friday, 23 May found me at Tullamarine airport in a state of eager anticipation. Collingwood were in the middle of a winning streak and coming off an upset win over the reigning champions, the mighty Brisbane Lions. Port were rated as genuine challengers for the flag — this was an exciting top of the table clash and I was going to be there! Oh, and I was going to see Dad as well!

I got to the airport with plenty of time to spare — well, I am a Virgo and I hate being late for anything. As I waited to check in, I noticed football colours everywhere. This wasn't really surprising as Collingwood were in Adelaide, Hawthorn in Perth and Essendon were due to play the much anticipated first game at Stadium Australia against the Sydney Swans. Of course the world is always black and white to me, but on this occasion, it seemed more so than usual. I got through the check-in with minimum fuss and then joined what seemed to be an even bigger line waiting for security. I looked ahead and saw another line converging with mine and thought 'they look familiar'. I swear my powers of observation never cease to impress me! Who looked familiar? I was staring at the all too familiar heads — very noticeable over the crowds — of Josh Fraser, Steve McKee and Anthony Rocca!

Well, this was interesting! At that moment I made a mistake that will be familiar to those of you who spend a lot of time on your own. I turned around and started muttering out loud about what I'd seen. You know the sort of thing. I turned to say, 'Looks like the Collingwood boys are on this flight.' Of course, the person behind me was going to be interested, weren't they? The words died on my tongue as I turned and looked into the eyes of Gavin Brown! Whoops! I guess he already knew that the Collingwood boys were on this flight. I wanted to disappear through the floor, but I suspect Brownie is used to people turning to jelly when they see him, and he just smiled and took it in his stride. I gathered myself together and managed to get through security without a fuss!

I had a thoroughly entertaining flight, courtesy of the Magpies floorshow. They were incredibly well-behaved, of course, but they moved around, talked to each other and ate! Oh yes they ate! In the process they confirmed my belief in the inedibility of most aircraft fare. Even though the boys had special high-carbohydrate meals prepared, they weren't going to take any chances and came on board equipped with bags of bread rolls, all made up. I remember Anthony Rocca eating a few — mind you he is a big boy!

I lost the boys once we landed at Adelaide. Then I was totally confused by the choice of conveyors and spent ten minutes waiting at the wrong one while my luggage racked up frequent flyer points on another. In the middle of this Dad arrived, slightly flustered for once. The reason for his disarray was clear; he'd had to fight his way through the thronging Adelaide media as he came into the airport. Apparently there was a footy team in town and everyone was interested!

'So Dad, who'll be in the box tonight?' Suddenly, I started to feel uneasy about the whole affair. First of all, Dad reeled off a list of business associates and clients, all of whom seemed to be Port Power fans. Then he told me to make sure I wore warm enough clothing for the night's game. 'But we're in the box, aren't we?' I said. Crushing blow number one: my vision of an MCG style Super Box was somewhat optimistic. In fact the 'box' was actually a partitioned-off section of seating in the open! Okay, the spirit of adventure was still there. And the box was placed in among the home team supporters! Oh oh! Things were starting to look somewhat shaky. I was with Dad's clients, all of whom were Port supporters, so I'd have to act with decorum — and one misplaced word was likely to bring the wrath of half the stand down on my head! Only one thing sustained me; Dad barracks for the Crows and hates the Power. Surely he'd be supporting me? Big mistake. The only team Dad hates more than the Power, is any one from Victoria!

Undaunted, I took my brave pills and prepared for the game. Out came the black-and-white garb (Well, my scarf, anyway.) I'm proud of my team and not afraid to show it. But, as Dad said, it looked like a Port scarf anyway!

We were due at the ground at 6.30 p.m. and Dad surprised me when he said we'd be leaving at 5.30 p.m. Now anyone with any knowledge of Adelaide will know that Football Park is not that far out of town, so I queried Dad's timing. He informed me, with a straight face, that we had to go early to avoid the traffic! Traffic? This is Adelaide, Dad! Well, he was right. Although we did get there with over half an hour to stand in the cold and rain until we were let in, we did beat a most impressive traffic jam on the Port Road coming in! Many supporters missed the first bounce because of it. It's a shame the Port Power boys weren't similarly afflicted! As we waited outside, I had the joy of seeing the Channel Nine commentary team arrive, including my hero, our President — Eddie McGuire! I noticed with some alarm that while Dermott Brereton and Garry Lyon were subject to a bit of stirring from the gathering hordes, Eddie copped a few sprays and some jostling. The natives were obviously restless and hungry for blood!

Finally, we got to the box and made ourselves comfortable. It was cosy to say the least, but once full we were certainly warm! Also, we were well catered for with a seemingly endless flow of hot and cold platters being passed around. My thanks to Jardines for their hospitality. As Dad's guests arrived, I noted the growing number of Power scarves and the maniacal gleam in their eyes. Dad kept introducing me as 'my daughter, the Collingwood supporter', much in the same way as Basil and Sybil Fawlty would say of Manuel — 'He's from Barcelona!'

Dad kept saying, 'After all, I'm a Crows supporter so I don't care who wins.' I might have been convinced, except for his almost encyclopaedic knowledge of the Port players and his obvious admiration for their simple training and warm-up drills! My fears of the surrounding crowd were soon confirmed as the sight of a Collingwood player on the big screen provoked boos, cat calls, and utterly unmentionable suggestions about their mother's morals that absolutely horrified me! I hadn't heard anything like it, not since the last days at Victoria Park anyway!

Nathan Buckley was singled out for a particularly vitriolic attack. I cannot say what was said about him; however if he'd done half of it I'm sure he'd be in jail now. Now it's not entirely a surprise that Bucks cops more than his fair share of abuse; it's a sad fact that the better a player is, the more he is targeted by the opposition. But Bucks is a Port Adelaide boy!

He won the Magarey Medal while playing for Port Adelaide! I asked one of my fellow guests why this was so and the answer was quite simple. Yes, he *was* a Port boy, and yes, they'd love to have him back. But he didn't come back, he stayed at Collingwood and I don't think they'll ever forgive him for that.

By quarter time, Collingwood were five goals down and the fight was just about out of me. I huddled in my little corner of the box, drank red wine, tried not to knock the food over and sulked as the exultant Power supporters told me all about it! Along with the Magpies, I revived in the second half and I have to admit that I found my voice as three-quarter time approached and we were only a goal behind.

The last quarter was a nightmare. The Pies had eight scoring shots to five while managing to go down by five points after Anthony Rocca's kick on the death knell went through for a behind — too many rolls and not enough goals Pebbles! My strangled cry of 'Oh f**k!' was mercifully covered by the ecstatic howls of the Port mob as the final siren went and their team stole the four points.

As you've probably realised, I'm not a good loser and I really struggled that night, particularly as, even through my misery, I knew that I had to behave myself for Dad. So, I was charming — honestly! I smiled when someone said it was a shame that one team had to lose … easy to say that when your team has won! I refrained from pointing out that the goal umpire was wearing coke-bottle glasses and that his guide dog had gone on strike for the night! I wasn't bitter — much! I did point out, somewhat prophetically as it turned out, that Port had better watch out because we'd get them in the finals — but I didn't really believe it. I really just wanted to cry! Once again I'd come to Footy Park and once again I'd seen victory snatched away at the last minute! And this time, there was no-one who cared!

We said goodnight to the guests and battled our way back to the car. Getting out of the car park was reminiscent of the old days at Waverley as we waited our turn to join the log jam on the road. Dad didn't gloat, but he didn't commiserate either. I decided not to re-live the game, the memories were too painful. So we listened to music and talked about other things.

Back at the flat, we caught the end of the game on the television as we sat with one last drink for the night. Funny thing about replays is they never change. Didn't matter how many times I watched Pebbles kick that shot, it missed the bloody goal posts every time! I turned away from the TV to say something to Dad and glimpsed a touch of satisfaction, even triumph, on his face! And then it hit me — he'd got me back! For the first time in our footy odyssey, he'd had the upper hand and been in control and I'd been out of it. And you know what? I didn't like it much. But I guess it was twenty years coming so I owed him that much.

The rest of the season saw Collingwood fighting with the Adelaide teams for spots in the top four and ultimately eliminating both of them from contention once September came! Dad took that pretty hard, especially the Preliminary Final loss. I have to say I thoroughly enjoyed the moment and may have rubbed it in just a little — okay, so three choruses of

'Good Old Collingwood Forever' on his Message Bank might have been a bit unnecessary but when I think of the times I listened to 'We're the pride of (bloody) South Australia'! … Throughout the disappointment of the finals, I sensed serenity in Dad which came from the belief that equilibrium had been found, and that I had paid for my past football sins!

So, Dad, I'll pay this one and we're even. Now what I'd like is to take you to the MCG, in front of 60,000 baying Magpies supporters, as we take apart the opposition! I'll shout you lunch! I'll buy you a drink! I'm out of my mind. Hell will freeze over or St Kilda will win a flag before Dad subjects himself to that.

At the end of the day, despite his deplorable taste in football teams, there is no doubt that I owe my love of sport, and for 'the game', to my dad. In fact, I can probably blame him for making me a Collingwood supporter. So thanks Dad — I think!

Robbie
Reverence

It happened on an otherwise inauspicious Saturday during the final school term in early spring 2001. It was a rather humid morning and Patrick, my then six-year-old son, was getting ready for his 9.00 a.m. swimming lesson. Patrick trotted out from his bedroom, having just dressed himself, wearing a Melbourne Demons football guernsey. Nothing unusual in that, of course. Patrick often put on his sleeveless Demons guernsey, the one with No. 33 on the back — the number of his then favourite player, his hero, Jeff Farmer. But it wasn't *his* sleeveless guernsey with *his* favourite player's number on the back that he was wearing. Rather it was *my* long-sleeved Demons jumper with *my* first-ever favourite player, my hero's number on the back!

Patrick was so pleased with himself saying, 'Look, Mum. It's your favourite player's jumper!' Well, I simply couldn't contain myself. I barked at him, 'What are you wearing that for? You can't wear that! That's my jumper!' Poor little fellow

— the incredulous look on his face. Patrick had no idea what he had done wrong; that he had done anything wrong.

'But I found it in *my* wardrobe!' Patrick defended himself, tears welling up.

'Yes, I know,' I was forced to admit. I had put it there myself when we moved into this house the previous January. I hadn't been able to fit into the jumper for years. It was a firm fit when I was given it at seventeen or eighteen years of age — that is about twenty years and ten kilos ago. I figured I was never going to be that slim again and, with some misgivings, decided Patrick might as well get some wear out of it … but for appropriately important occasions, please! I hadn't intended for Patrick to wear the jumper around the house or down to the pool, otherwise I would have put it in his chest of drawers where it would have been obvious that he was meant to find it, wouldn't I?

Bruce attempted to moderate the rapidly escalating hysteria. 'Hey, it *was* in his wardrobe, you know?'

'Of course I know — *I* put it there!' I grumped back. Bruce, well aware that I hadn't yet consumed my ritual morning coffee, trod warily.

'Um, so, ah … why did you put it there, Pen, if you don't want Paddy to wear it?'

'Well!' I gasped, disbelieving that my own husband could possibly fail to appreciate the reverence which I accorded that guernsey and wishing that after twelve years of marriage he could at least make some effort to learn to read my mind. 'It's not that I don't want him to wear it,' I tried to explain, impatiently. 'It's just that I don't want him to wear it … around … you know, on weekends. It's more for special events, like going to the footy or party dress-ups. Anyway, it's too hot for Patrick to wear a long-sleeved jumper today … and not to the pool, for goodness sake! It's too easy to lose stuff there!'

'But I *really, really* want to wear it!' protested Patrick with his usual response when he really, really wanted something.

'Just because you really want something doesn't mean that you should always get it, does it Patrick?' I retorted with my usual response to my son's 'I really, really want …' paddy.

Bruce, sensing that there was perhaps more to this than met the eye — that is, more than my usual grumpy mood prior to my first coffee for the day — was determined to nip things in the bud before anything was said that would be hard to forgive, let alone forget. 'Patrick, you can wear the jumper another time but Mum would rather you not wear it now. It's too hot to wear a jumper today anyway, okay?'

'But I *really, really, really* want to wear it!' pleaded Patrick again, tears rolling down his cheeks now.

'I know and you *can* wear it, just not today,' reiterated Bruce. After more protests and pleading from the ankle-biter, bearing puffy eyes and blotchy red face (so like his mother when upset, poor little man!), he was eventually shuffled out the door and cajoled down to the Recreation Centre by his dad, just in time for his lesson.

Well, what a killjoy! I felt like such a crabby old bag for having deprived my son of the untold pleasure of wearing his mother's football guernsey — which she was, in fact, unable to wear herself any more. A guernsey that represented my favourite football player as a teenager — the legendary Melbourne Football Club champion, Robert Flower, complete with his favoured long-sleeves and famous No. 2 on the back.

Oh Robbie, what a player you were!

I sat, now with my precious caffeinated beverage in hand, and pondered my mixed feelings about Patrick's fixation on wanting to wear my Robbie Flower guernsey. I didn't suppose I had thought much about what it would be like to have kids when I was growing up, but I certainly would never have expected that a child of mine would be remotely interested in any of my childhood or teenhood heroes. Who is ever as keen on their parents' heroes as their parents were? I'm not sure I even knew whom my parents admired when I was Patrick's age. The realisation suddenly swept over me that I was very lucky to have a son like Patrick. I was so proud of him for many reasons, but right then I felt honoured; honoured that he had not only chosen my football club to support but was also interested, if not fascinated, in the history of my club and its players. I marvelled at Patrick's knowledge, precocious for his tender years, about my first ever football hero. Patrick had heard much about Robbie from me, of course. He had also read about him in his rapidly expanding library of football history books and endlessly viewed videos (how they bring back memories!) of my hero playing for the Melbourne Demons.

My hero. Those two little words have such a respectful, even reverential, ring to them. Particularly when applied to the admiration and esteem in which I have always held Robbie Flower. Calling him 'Robbie' actually sounds just the opposite, really — a bit irreverent, babyish even, for such a sublime player. I promise I'll try to remember to call you 'Robert' from now on, Robbie. (Oops!) I'm sure he wouldn't mind. Robbie Flower has always been such a genuinely nice guy.

Funny, I mused. Thinking about Robbie Flower is, for me, a bit like recalling a fairytale. I was ten years old in 1973 when Robbie started his career with Melbourne. He was a skinny, unassuming teenager — he certainly didn't look to have the body of a good footballer, let alone a great one. Actually, Robbie probably didn't look much different when he retired in 1987 — he was just as wiry but had a few more laughter lines. Robbie wasn't exactly what I would call handsome, either. He wasn't bad looking, mind you, just not what I would call 'pin-up material'. Having said that it certainly didn't stop me from lining my walls with posters of Robbie. (I wish I had known about Blu-tack then; moving the posters around wasn't too good for the paintwork.) I bet you are thinking, 'Oh, you must have had the hots for Robbie to put posters of him all over your walls!' But I didn't, honestly. I admired and adored Robbie and thought he was the best foot-ball player ever, but I don't remember that I ever fantasised about him (if you know what I mean). Actually, I even used to hide behind my wardrobe doors when I was getting dressed. How ridiculously paranoid I know, but his eyes seemed to follow me around the room.

Anyway, that skinny teenager had the silkiest of football skills right from the outset, and his skill was matched by his sense of fair play. Robbie was agile, fast, and he moved with a smoothness and grace that mesmerised the fans and deceived his opposition. Robbie always took the ball cleanly, whether marking or hand-passing, and his delivery to team-mates by both foot and hand was accurate and consistent. Robbie was

legendary for his long runs with the ball up the wing —
bouncing here, bouncing there, and all the while weaving a
pathway through the defenders. Robbie had an uncanny ability to control the ball; his apparent effortlessness has been
likened to having 'the ball on a string' as if it were a yo-yo.
Robbie lacked a big hard body but he certainly lacked nothing
in the way of endeavour for the ball. Robbie was respected
equally well by those he played against as well as with.

I remember sitting in front of the box with my late father
watching the football highlights on a Saturday evening before
the news, and he would say things like, 'Flower has more skill
than the rest of that team put together!' It was definitely a
compliment for Robbie, but probably also a bit of a back-
hander for the rest of the team as Melbourne rarely finished
in, or even near, the top half of the ladder during my teen
years. The fairytale aspect of my memories definitely had
more (in fact, everything) to do with watching *Robbie* play as
opposed to watching my *team* play.

I was feeling nostalgic and thinking that I would love to
pull out and read an essay that I might have written about the
sensational Robbie Flower when I was at secondary school. A
500 word English exercise along the lines, 'Describe your hero
and explain what it is that you so admire about him or her?'
It might have started something like:

> My Hero — Flower of My Heart (*Aargh! Too mushy.*)
> My Hero — Petal Power (*Yuck, worse.*)
> My Hero — Flower Power! (*Very seventies! Perfect!*)

In a country town far, far away where the local football team was called the Buchan Cavemen, there was a girl who followed the Melbourne Demons in the Victorian Football League. The girl was lonely because no-one else followed the Demons and, besides, they all thought the team was useless as it languished at the bottom of the ladder. But the girl knew that her team was not useless, not least because it provided the opportunity for one of the best footballers of all time to showcase his impeccable skills and audacious talent. The girl was Penny Mackieson and the footballer, her hero, was Robbie Flower ...

I don't have the best memory in the world but I'm sure, even though I have thought about it a lot over the years, I never did write an essay like that (I had a good look when we moved recently and turned up nothing). Still, I wanted to read something to remind me of my hero's feats, in all their glory. I gazed at the bookcase in the study and noticed a substantial gap in the football section. 'Hmmmpf,' I said out loud to myself. 'I bet Patrick has got *The Clubs* out again!' It had been a slow process teaching Patrick that not all the football books in the house belonged to him. While I'm sure he knew that *The Clubs* was my book, he often forgot to ask me if he could take it from the shelf and have a read, and he rarely ever remembered to put it back when he had finished with it.

I rummaged around the house looking on tables and chairs, picking up piles of books and loose papers that seemed to breed wherever Patrick set himself down. Finally, success. *The Clubs* lay open under a few sheets of scrap paper on which Patrick had written a series of dates and football scores — he had probably jotted them down when performing one of his epic commentaries on some of the great Melbourne Grand Finals of the 1950s. The book was open on page 256, the page that happened to have a tribute to Robbie Flower written by John Ross — the page I was intending to search for on locating the book. I started to read, taking mental notes, and nodding in agreement as I pictured Robbie in action. I doubted that I could have written more accurate or succinct words to describe what I so admired about my hero …

Robbie Flower — the Ultimate Demon

Robbie Flower was a beautiful player to watch. Few players have given supporters more pleasure or wreaked more havoc. He was graceful and elusive, with a long penetrating kick and he could mark high above the pack.

A slight, unassuming man with glasses, the young Robert Flower would have hardly bred fear in the opposition had they seen him enter the dressing rooms. He began playing in the Seniors as a 17-year-old schoolboy in 1973, scoring a goal in his first game, and he stayed there, a fixture for the next 15 years and 272 games. During those years, Melbourne had six coaches, and frequently finished in the doldrums, but when all else was bleak, it was always worth going to watch Robbie in action.

To the delight of the supporters, he would take off for a run in front of the Members' Stand, leaving his opponent in his wake as he turned, baulked and skilfully evaded all comers. Then he would pass, hitting his team-mate on the chest. He was a champion who made the game look easy. And always he played the ball. He won the admiration of those he played against as well as his team-mates through his skill and fair play.

Robbie Flower was the definitive wingman, though Ron Barassi was one coach who liked to move him around. He played him on a half-back flank and was booed by the supporters who had come, after all, partly to watch Robbie fire. But fire he did, in whatever position he was played. He captained the team from 1981 and, in his final years, played mostly on the half-forward flank, a position in which he was deadly.

To the bewilderment of Melbourne supporters, Flower never won the Brownlow Medal. Few players have fitted so aptly the description of 'fairest and best'.

His career ended in 1987, when Melbourne came within a kick of a Grand Final. His fragile build made him injury prone in his later years, but always he was an inspiration to the team. He is still very much a part of Melbourne and its plans for a bright future.[9]

It was indeed always worth
going to watch the graceful and elusive
Robbie in action.

The very first VFL match I ever attended was on another otherwise inauspicious Saturday. It was a Hawthorn versus Melbourne match at Waverley Park — in 1980, I think. I must admit I'm not sure about the year, but I am sure about how Robbie played that day.

Melbourne lost the match but it was not for the want of Robbie's efforts. One magic piece of play (long burned deep in my brain) started with Robbie causing a turnover somewhere around the half-back line. He took off and dodged around an opposition player. He bounced the ball, baulked around another Hawk, took a second bounce and was shepherded by team-mates as he sprinted up the flank past the centre of the ground. The crowd hushed. I had lost count of the number of bounces then, just as Robbie was about to kick long towards the top of our goal square, one red-and-blue clad supporter yelled out a heartfelt, 'Don't give it to him Robbie! Go all the way!'

I had absolutely no idea what the supporter was on about … until the ball, beautifully delivered from Robbie's boot while on the run, bounced off the chest of the Melbourne forward who had been calling for it. There was a bit of a scramble, then a Hawthorn player crumbed the ball and cleared it from our forward zone. The ball moved quickly to the other end of the ground with apparently little resistance from our players, and Hawthorn scored yet another goal. Robbie hadn't stopped running after his kick, but he was puffing hard after his long run and was at least a kick behind play by the time Hawthorn had cleared the ball from our forward area. I laughed out loud to myself as I recalled the light-bulb moment when I grasped the full meaning of the supporter's advice; you'll have to win the ball, maintain possession of it all the way up the ground and then kick a goal yourself! The other Melbourne players were not to be trusted with the ball, no matter how well Robbie delivered it to them. This fact was confirmed for me repeatedly throughout the remainder of that match and dozens that followed, just as that famous one-liner, 'Don't give it to him, Robbie!', was repeated on countless occasions by Melbourne supporters.

I flicked around the Melbourne section of *The Clubs* and was surprised to find that Robbie was the MFC leading goal-kicker on four occasions but won the best and fairest award only once, in 1977. 'He was robbed,' I thought. 'Robbie was robbed ... of his own club's best and fairest awards, just as he had been of the League's best and fairest award.' All of my football-following friends (even the Collingwood supporters!) agree that Robbie Flower *would* have been a very worthy recipient of the Brownlow Medal and, in fact, *should* have won it on *at least* one occasion. Melbourne had two Brownlow Medallists during the period of Robbie's career; Brian Wilson (1982) and Peter Moore (1984). In my opinion, they weren't even in the same 'league' as Robbie. Let's face it, Robbie's career performances lived up to the meaning of his name, according to the Oxford Dictionary, anyway. 'flower. noun ... best part, pick (of)'. Robbie was definitely the best player in my team ... the pick of the Demons players.

Robbie still holds the MFC record for the most number of games played — 272. The record looked set to be broken by Steven Febey in season 2002, but a persistent injury worry led to his mid-season retirement instead. I lamented that Robbie never got to play in a Grand Final let alone a Premiership match for Melbourne, either. Robbie missed out on playing in Melbourne's Night Premiership match against Essendon in 1987 due to injury. The Demons made it to the VFL Grand Final the very next year after Robbie retired. I was there at the MCG that day. We lost badly to Hawthorn. How painfully familiar. Tears started to fill my eyes though, as I read on ...

A Tough Task for Robbie

The winning Hawthorn players were presented with their 1988 Premiership medals by the recently retired Melbourne champion Robbie Flower. He performed with his usual grace.[10]

Enough with the nostalgia, I thought, trying hard to suppress the sadness threatening to overwhelm me. Quick, I needed a distraction. Almost 10.00 a.m. The boys were due home from swimming any minute. I started to prepare some morning tea for them and was relieved to be feeling much better than before they had left. Reflecting on Robbie had led me to viewing my earlier altercation with Patrick in a new light, a more mellow light.

The proud Demons supporter in me said, 'Surely Patrick wanting to wear my Robbie Flower jumper is a reflection of his respect for that great player; of his pride in such a grand past champion for the Melbourne Demons, Patrick's and my team, *our* team. How many other kids of Patrick's age are as interested as he is in the past champions of their chosen football club? I should be encouraging my son to enjoy a piece of living memorabilia by wearing my jumper. I should even try to get Robbie to sign it at a club function some time. Fancy being annoyed with Patrick over this!'

On the other hand, however, the frustrated mother in me said, 'But Patrick is only six and he hasn't yet learned to take care of his possessions, particularly his clothes — not even his favourite ones. Why, at a barbecue at school earlier that year Patrick let some kids he had only just met bury his favourite wrestling characters in the sand pit then walked away and forgot about them until it was pack-up time, when I asked him where they were. All right, he was only five then, but Patrick still needed to learn that when you value something you should take special care of it.

So I felt somewhat affirmed that my decision for the Robbie Flower jumper to be worn only on special occasions was the correct one. If Patrick truly respected the player, my hero, he could jolly well learn some respect for that jumper — my jumper! I didn't really *give* it to him, you know; I just *loaned* it so he could get some wear out of it before he also grew too big to fit into it. Lucky we can never grow out of our heroes, can we?

I also felt rather guilty about the way in which I had delivered my ruling to Patrick earlier on. Before I had any more time to think about how to make amends, in bustled Patrick and Bruce, all fresh and squeaky clean from the shower. 'We got these sweets to share with you, Mum,' offered Patrick. A peace offering from my little man, I thought. What a sweetie, indeed!

'Thank you, Paddy,' I responded. (Notice the use of his nickname as an expression of endearment now?) 'I'm sorry I was cross at you this morning about wanting to wear my Robbie Flower jumper, mate. I did put it in your wardrobe for you to wear but only for special occasions, okay?'

'Okay, Mum,' said Paddy, without any further ado.

And everything was okay. I was back in Paddy's good books, just where I like to be. Paddy was back in my pocket, just where I like him to be. And Robbie was still up on a pedestal, right where he will always be!

What's He Done This Time?

I remember 7 October 1991 with a horrible clarity. It started like any other Monday; grunts and groans of protest as the body realised another working week was starting. Listen to the news on the radio as I snatch that extra five minutes in bed. Through the morning ritual of shower, dress and make-up before running to the bus and from there the train. A careful perusal of the paper (nowhere near as interesting now that the footy season is over) and a disturbed snooze as the train gets closer to the city. Finally, wake up all over again as I stagger from Parliament station and purchase the coffee that will start my flagging system and so to the office to the files that I hoped would miraculously disappear over the weekend.

Nothing seemed abnormal that particular Monday, as I sat and planned my day. I enjoyed the half hour or so in the office before the rest of the team arrived; it gave me the opportunity to focus and plan before the inevitable phone calls started. I had plenty to do and was quickly absorbed in my work.

Consciously or sub-consciously, I became aware that the other guys were arriving. About 9.00 a.m. I remember sitting up ready to properly acknowledge my co-workers and compare weekend notes over another cup of tea. Just at that moment the last of the team, Mark Edmonds, came in; as always, the *Sun* under his arm and a startled and sleepy air about him. 'How was the weekend? Did you watch Bathurst? Did I really drink that much on Friday night?' You know the stuff — questions that were being repeated in thousands of offices on every Monday of the year. Trouble is, this one was so different.

Mark looked more diffident than normal. He looked at me like a man who wished he was anywhere but there at that moment and said, 'Have you heard about Darren Millane?'

'No,' I said, not really concentrating, 'what's he done this time?'

'He's dead!'

I sat and looked at him, at the office, at the alley wall outside the window, and I didn't see any of them. I'd expected any answer but that one. Tried to play Reg Varney on an interstate bus? Yes. Punched some loud mouth in a pub? Possibly. But, dead? Pants couldn't be dead. The man who had played out the 1990 finals series with a broken thumb had to be indestructible, didn't he?

I'd become an active Collingwood supporter again during 1990, largely because, in Tracey, I had found someone to go to the football and worship a whole new set of heroes with. Of all the heroes I discovered in 1990 two were to stand out — Gavin Brown (probably the favourite of every Collingwood supporter at that time) and Darren Millane. Other people have described Darren's skills and ability and have encapsulated his style much better than I can ever hope to. All I can say is that I've never seen a player who seemed to have so much time and space when he had the ball. While famous for his pack-bursting goals, it's that element of space that I recall most. He had, without doubt, the greatest sense of presence that I've ever seen on a football field and, without doubt, every Collingwood player walked taller when he was on the ground.

Every football fan knows the details of that dreadful day. For me, the day was spent as a sleep walker as I numbly pieced together the story and tried to come to terms with the loss. I remember colleagues calling from as far away as Perth asking how I felt and wanting to talk about what had happened. In the corridors and tea rooms of the office, as in corridors and tea rooms all over Melbourne, the conversation was only of one thing — Pants is dead! Watching the news that night, hearing the details of the accident and its cause, was a nightmare. Other Collingwood fans may not appreciate me saying this, but my initial reaction was anger at the stupidity and irresponsibility he showed by getting behind the wheel in that state. I cannot condone that action and the only saving grace is that no-one else was injured or killed. As the week went on, my anger protected me to some extent and I believed I had my emotions under control.

I hadn't, of course. I was tested on Friday evening, when we called in on friends and the conversation turned, as conversations all over Melbourne were turning, to Millane's death. My friend told me that her Carlton-supporting,

Collingwood-hating (is there any other kind) father had sent a sympathy card to Darren's family. I was surprised and asked why. Apparently her father hated Collingwood with a passion, but remembered that when his Collingwood-loving grandson had been terminally ill with cancer, it had been Darren who had come to visit him — not just once as asked, but several times. Also, when he lost the battle, Millane had attended the funeral. His grandfather felt that the least he could was to return some of the respect and compassion shown by Darren back to his family at this dark time. Slowly the protective shell that I'd kept around me all week began to crumble as I faced the impact that Darren had made on so many people, not just as a footballer, but as a man. That a rabid (is there any other kind?) Carlton supporter was touched so deeply by a Collingwood hero shook me. How, then, were the faithful coping?

I found out when I turned on the news that night to face reports of Millane's funeral. The sight of tens of thousands of 'ordinary' people lining the streets of Dandenong and congregating outside the Town Hall proved how much he had meant to so many. A year earlier, after Collingwood's historic win in the 1990 Grand Final, a reporter had said that as he looked around the world had turned black and white. So it was on this day — only so much blacker. It is believed to be the largest crowd at a funeral for a public figure in Victoria's history. This may be hard to believe but some Dandenong business people told me after the event that they had never seen anything like it in their lives. The centre of town was shut down and roads in and out were closed. Every community group was represented. A small boy sobbed on his father's shoulders, grandmothers in lovingly knitted Collingwood cardigans and jumpers stood sad-eyed holding on to the hands of their daughters and granddaughters, businessmen and women in suits unashamedly wept at the passing of one of their own.

And then there were the players. As Darren's coffin was carried out by his blood brothers and playing brothers, we caught sight of his team-mates — Brownie, Ned, Mick, Banks — all looked ravaged with grief and battling to come to terms with such a shocking reality. As the famous No. 42 appeared and 'Good Old Collingwood Forever' was heard, I lost it. A week of suppressing my feelings of loss, of masking it with anger rather than grief, took its toll. I sat in the lounge room and wept uncontrollably — I had never responded that way to the loss of someone who I did not know personally, but Darren personified all that had made me so proud to be a Collingwood supporter.

> He was talented, tough, passionate, and individual and he took no shit from anyone.

No-one ever beat Darren — no-one but himself, in the end.

Inevitably, the funeral wasn't the end of the tributes to Darren. At the Copeland Trophy presentation (previously a triumphant stage for the flamboyant star) an award was initiated in his name for the best Team Mate. What a fitting compliment to a man who gave it all for his team and club. Gavin Brown was the inaugural winner of the award and his words summed up the respect and love with which Darren was held. 'Of all my trophies, this will be the one that means the most to me.' Then the club captain, Tony Shaw, gave his own tribute. Tony isn't the most eloquent of public speakers but I still recall his words, spoken more than ten years ago, and they still cause my scalp to prickle — 'If any of you need more than the mention of his name to do your best for this club then you don't belong at Collingwood!' What a tribute! What a man!

Over the summer the pain started to lessen. I bought the tribute video and watched as Eddie McGuire kept his personal grief in limbo to pay a warm tribute to his lost friend.

Then came the first home and away game against the Brisbane Bears at Victoria Park. The club had decreed that there would be a supporters' tribute and the supporters responded. The banner that day read 'We'll do it in '92 for 42' — simple but to the point. When the players ran on they lined up for a minute's silence in Darren's honour. I must say I have been party to any number of similar tributes at football games (every Anzac Day) but I have never known such an all-enveloping silence in all my life. No wally felt a need to yell out or cheer, no trains went past and the birds even stopped singing. Eyes were dabbed, noses blown and five months of sorrow had a communal release in a place where no-one would censor and everyone would understand. In the ultimate tribute to the competitive player, Collingwood went on to flog Brisbane by some eleven goals!

Over the years, the spirit and memory of Pants has never strayed from the club. Unfortunately we didn't 'do it in '92 for 42' — we were knocked out of the finals by St Kilda in the first week.

And the years since have not all been vintage ones for the proud club. Without doubt, the loss of Millane has affected the club in any number of ways. The club has taken a hard line on players who go astray off the field, particularly those who enjoy too much of the amber fluid — or any other colour for that matter! On the field, Collingwood has struggled for an enforcer — not a thug, but a player who makes the opposition look over their shoulders and makes his team-mates walk a little taller. It's the fact that we've only made the finals three times since his loss.

When I started this chapter, my plan was to stop with the 1992 tribute at Victoria Park. This changed, however, after attending the 2001 Copeland Trophy Night. As I looked around and reflected on a year that had promised so much, and promised so much more for the future, I realised that we were finally putting Darren's loss behind us. Collingwood's community partnership with the TAC and the involvement of Magpies team members in youth driving education programs brings a full circle to the loss of our greatest star (and the years of humiliating stories about Collingwood players being caught doing drink-affected misdemeanours).

There is a new generation of players at Collingwood who are ready to make heroes of themselves and, we hope, to reach the ultimate prize as Darren and his team-mates did in 1990. We also have a player who embodies much of Darren's spirit on field and causes the opposition (and his own players on occasions) to look over their shoulders. He too is talented, tough, passionate, individual and he takes no shit from anyone. I am of course referring to the 'D-9', Jarrod Molloy, who has embodied the spirit of Victoria Park like a ten year veteran. It was fitting that Jarrod won the 2001 Darren Millane award. It was even more fitting that it was presented by Collingwood's favourite son and Darren's close friend, Gavin Brown, along with Darren's always dignified mother, Denise. As he received the award, Jarrod spoke of Millane and Brownie as his former heroes and of the honour he felt to be at Collingwood and to receive the award. He also spoke of the future, of the youngsters in the team and how far they could go. In his speech, we could see the past, the present and the future of the club. The past was rocky, the present is good and the future will be great.

We can lay Darren to rest now. We need to look to the future, not seek comfort in the past. But he'll always be with us — as long as Collingwood is there.

I Dream of Football, Philosophy and The Universe

Awareness spread slowly through my body. I could see only brownness. Correction. Actually it was blackness flecked with exploding stars and fiery streaks of gold. Whatever. My eyes were still sealed firmly shut as they had been during my slumber. My body was aching, some parts of it anyway, and I was afraid to move. I knew I was seated but in what sort of position? My neck was stiff so I guessed that my head must be tilted somewhat awkwardly. My mouth and lips were uncomfortably dry. My mouth must have been open for some time. Where was I? The desert? That strange noise I heard a few minutes ago, was it a camel snoring or breaking wind? My own snoring, perhaps. In any event, that was definitely *not* what had disturbed my sleep.

But what had disturbed my sleep? Whatever it was had made me tense. Very tense. I tried to raise my eyelids; they felt heavy like steel shutters with only the flimsy strings of a Roman blind to manipulate them. I licked my lips and hoped the bitter taste in my mouth would go away. The sound of the motor as the car made its way along the freeway droned on. I was more awake now and remembered where I was. It was late Sunday afternoon (Sunday, 9 September 2001, to be precise). We were returning to Melbourne from a weekend visit to my mother in Bairnsdale. Bruce was driving and Patrick was in the back seat. Patrick must be engrossed in a book, I thought, as there was no talking. I adjusted my sunglasses and looked around to get my bearings. We were roughly two-thirds of the way home, a bit more than an hour's travel to go. I guessed that I must have nodded off with the afternoon sun beating in on me through the front windscreen. I reached for the water bottle. I was reminded all too well why I have always hated napping during the day; the nauseous feeling on waking up and that disgusting aftertaste that still lingered in my mouth.

But I had to concentrate to remember why my nap had been disturbed. What was that last thought I had been muddling over before starting to wake? Something on a whiteboard about planets and stars colliding ... the universe, maybe? Something else to do with pyramids, but not ancient Egyptian pyramids? And footballers ... AFL footballers ... Melbourne Football Club players ... my club's players! What?

I sipped on my bottle of spring water and suddenly it all came together. I had a dream. A rather interesting dream. It had no doubt been fed by my weariness after the travel and happenings of the weekend, my unplanned nap in the warmth of the front seat of the car, not to mention the sweets we had gobbled down during our journey before I had nodded off. Snakes! Yes, I think we had been eating snakes, of the 'sweets' variety, of course.

Back to more important things. The dream. Ah, yes, the dream! I had received an invitation from Neale Daniher, coach of the Melbourne Football Club no less, to speak to the players during the pre-season about the importance of maintaining a balance in their lives. Neale had allocated a two-hour session for this purpose.

Well, that was a fairly reasonable request, I thought. I am a social worker by profession and I have done a bit of training here and there. Of course, I had agreed to waive my usual fee for MFC. I figured that I knew a fair bit, both personally and professionally, about the need to balance the various aspects of one's life, including physical, emotional and psychological needs. And I could imagine how easy it might be for young blokes, who are training very hard in their chosen professional sport (or alternatively partying pretty hard thanks to their new found fame and fortune), to lose perspective on other aspects of their lives, particularly if they are living away from their families for the first time. They could easily neglect their non-physical needs to the ultimate detriment of their sporting and team performances, and their personal lives.

But I'd never done any sports psychology type work before. In fact, I hadn't even done any clinical social work for years — more than ten years! And why would Neale Daniher invite *me* to give a presentation to the players? Even though Neale 'Rowdy' Daniher took an engineering class at university with Bruce, I'm sure Neale wouldn't have said boo to Bruce or even have known who he was, let alone me (I wasn't even dating Bruce then). Maybe the connection is through Brian 'Choco'

Royal, now assistant coach of MFC. I knew Brian's wife, Maree, from our school days at Bairnsdale High School; we were in the same year, and sometimes the same class. But I think I had already left Bairnsdale for university when Maree and Brian got together. I certainly never met, much less knew, Brian then. In any event, I hadn't even seen Maree for years! Oh well, it was a dream, I suppose.

The next thing I remember is being introduced by Neale to the MFC players, then me standing in front of them to get the session underway. I remember feeling rather awestruck and very nervous. In real life I no doubt would have sat down with Neale and the other coaching staff to clarify the objectives of the session well in advance then gone away and prepared some stuff, sat down again with the coaching staff for feed-back, gone away again to make any adjustments, then provided a final copy of the session plan and support mater-ials to Neale well prior to the day's session. This detail wasn't covered in the dream (not surprisingly) so I don't know whether I was supposed to have been well prepared or not.

But I do know that the session wasn't just a presentation — it was very interactive. I remember thinking during my dream that these boys didn't know anything at all about me or what I might be able to offer them, and they were prob-ably thinking the session was a bit dorky anyway. So I'd have to make it as interesting as possible. Besides, the idea was for them to learn things about themselves and each other so I'd have to make sure that they did most of the work, with me as the facilitator as opposed to a boring old teacher. Old? Yes, technically I was old enough to be a mother to some of my audience. Why on earth would I be nervous, then?

Standing up in front of forty or so young,
fit, professional footballers
who happen to play for my club —
you've got to be kidding!

Not nervous? I was a wreck.

I got straight into the warm-up exercise (in my dream, of course). The best cure for nerves was surely to do something — those words, 'Do something! Do, do … don't think!' have surely been immortalised (at least in my mind) by John Kennedy, legendary former Premiership coach for Hawthorn Football Club in that *100 Years of Australian Football* video, which I swear Patrick has watched 200 times already.

Anyway, I paired off the players by writing all the guernsey numbers (1–40) on small pieces of paper, which were folded and placed in a hat, then asking David Neitz, the captain, and Andrew Leoncelli, one of the vice-captains, to each draw out a number thereby randomly assigning the pairs. There was an odd number of players present as Jeff Farmer wasn't there — I supposed he was spending time with his family in Western Australia. (And how prophetic! Within just a few weeks of my strange dream, it was announced that Farmer was leaving the Melbourne Demons to join the Fremantle Dockers from season 2002). So I made up the last pair with David Neitz, who just happens to be my favourite player! (That surely confirmed it was a dream.)

I asked the group to each think of the best thing, or one of the best things, that had ever happened to him in his lifetime, and to tell their partner what it was and why.

'It might be a football related experience or it might not. It doesn't matter what sphere of your life it comes from so long as you are happy to share it with the entire group via the person with whom you are paired.'

My pair kicked off with my favourite footballer telling the group about my favourite boy's birth.

'Penny says the best thing that has happened to her — apart from meeting me, of course' (*laughter and quips from the group*), 'was her first child. Penny and her husband, Bruce, had been trying to conceive a baby for some years ...' (*knowing looks and giggles*), '... when, in her early thirties, Penny became pregnant. The pregnancy went well, but the birth had to be induced after Penny's blood pressure went up around the time the baby was due to be born. Penny had a brief seven-and-a-half-hour labour ... Bruce was there the whole time giving her moral support.' (*Some laughter and more quips.*)

'The labour ended with a difficult mid-forceps delivery. To get this in perspective, it might be helpful to think of a mid-forceps delivery compared with an ordinary delivery as being like a dislocated shoulder versus a dislocated end joint on your little finger ...' (*Oohs and aahs from the other boys.*)

'They called the baby Patrick. He was average sized and healthy, but he had some injuries to his face from the forceps, which have become permanent scars. Penny had to have lots of stitches as a result of the birth' (*more oohs and aahs*), 'but she was very relieved and very proud to have given birth to a healthy baby — a first grandchild for both sides of the family. Penny reckons Patrick is a sensational kid, now six years old and not so little, and she and Bruce, all his family, in fact, are very proud of him. Oh, Penny's even more proud because he is a Melbourne member too.' *(Cheers and cheeky comments from the group.)*

Even in a dream, I have the need to share the gory details of my pregnancy and birthing experiences and brag about my beautiful child. Is it just me or is it gender related? And wouldn't you think I'd be too embarrassed to tell my favourite footballer, who also happens to be the captain of the oldest AFL club, one of the most successful in history? Well, I wasn't. I wasn't even embarrassed when it was shared with all the other players. This was definitely a dream. Strange then that I would still feel so nervous …

Anyway, the process of feeding back to the larger group was a lot of fun. The players' experiences ranged from educational milestones and football accolades to family and partner events, creative works, cars and travel. Most stories were somewhat embellished by the person doing the telling, though it was difficult to tell which as everyone seemed to immerse themselves in the exercise. When everyone had shared their partner's experiences, I asked the boys what they had learned from the exercise.

There were several humorous comments along the lines of, 'If only I had known that before!' and 'I knew I shouldn't have trusted him with my experience!' However, the players quickly identified that people's perceptions of their best experiences (whether individual or team) were usually ones they had had to work really hard for (i.e. make adjustments, at least, and often sacrifices; suffer some pain whether physical or emotional; stay focused) and were subsequently able to savour their achievements with others, whether it be friends, partner, family members, team-mates, and even their partner in the context of this exercise.

We moved on to a discussion about where football and football players fit in relation to the wider community. With the help of a whiteboard and red and blue whiteboard markers, I drew a pyramid.

ME: I would expect that you have all seen this diagram as a food pyramid in relation to your nutrition and dietary requirements. What is each layer comprised of?

PAUL WHEATLEY: Cereals, breads, fruit and veggies are at the bottom. You're supposed to eat more of those.

ME: Good answer from the man whose name sounds like a cereal brand!

A few giggles from the group.

JEFF WHITE: Dairy products, white meat, lean red meat and eggs are the things you should eat next most of.

ME: Yep. 'Whitey' coloured foods.

More giggles.

BRENT GRGIC: Fats and oils, sugar … and salt … are what you should eat least of.

ME: Aha. Otherwise you might feel a bit sick! (*A cheeky comment from Stephen Powell, 'A purge from Gerge!, followed by much laughter from the group.*) Anything else?

RUSSELL ROBERTSON: Where do nuts fit in?

A few very cheeky comments and uproarious laughter.

ME: Takes one to know one, right? On top of the pack, I mean pyramid, but not quite up with the fats and oils and stuff. Does that sound right, everyone?

Affirming nods from the group.

ME: Okay. This pyramid provides a framework for understanding what foods we need a lot of through to what foods we need little of. Thinking of it from another perspective, the framework can be considered a 'hierarchy' that represents the most potent foods or nutritional sources at the top, that is those you need fewest of, through to the least potent at the bottom, or those you need most of. We can use the same framework to depict Melbourne Football Club. Where do you reckon you blokes, the players, fit?

I draw another pyramid beside the food pyramid.

RUSSELL ROBERTSON: On top, of course!

Chuckles and nods from the group.

ME: Okay, and where are the coaching staff.

SHANE WOEWODIN: Oh, they would probably be the next layer down.

ME: The trainers and other support staff? What about the recruiters?

GUY RIGONI: Yeah, they're all next.

ME: What about the Board? Where does it sit in the pyramid?

There was discussion about where the Board should sit; alongside the team, the coaching staff, or down with the supporters. The group eventually decided that the Board was a sub-set of the club membership and the latter sit above MFC fans that are non-members. The bottom layer comprised football fans in general.

ME: Okay. You've placed yourselves — the players, the people who *receive* the most amount of money *from* the club — at the top of the hierarchy. You've put the members, the people who *give* their money *to* the club to pay you blokes, towards the bottom. And the various other paid club managers and support staff are somewhere in the middle. I think we forgot the sponsors. Where would you put them?

STEVEN FEBEY: Alongside the club members and the Board, maybe?

ME: All right. Let's just take a minute to look at the pyramid we've constructed. What do you think it reflects? To use the hierarchy analogy of before, does it indicate *who* is most important to the success of the club in descending order?

PETER WALSH: I think it does in a way, but it's a bit of a problem having the 'nuts' towards the top. *Laughter from the group.* They're not necessarily the most important just because you don't need as many of them as in the other groups.

ME: Great point! And it highlights exactly why I don't like to use a pyramid, certainly not one that points this way up, to represent where individuals fit into an organisation. In the Department of Human Services, where I was employed directly and indirectly for some fourteen years or so, the direct service staff and lower level supervisors and managers always liked to draw the organisational hierarchy like this (*drawing an inverted pyramid on the whiteboard as I talked*).

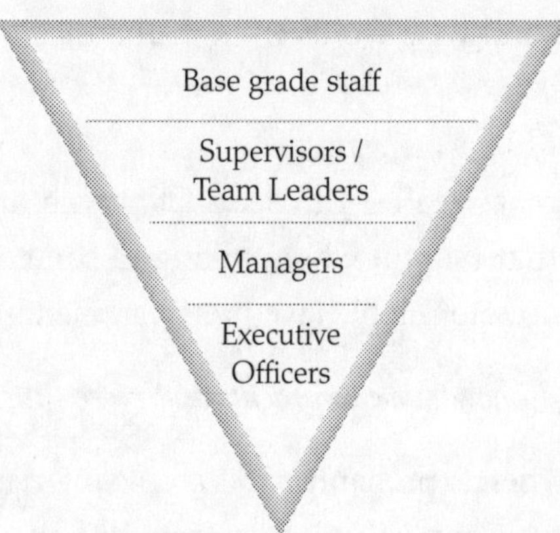

ME: The theory is that it is the lower level staff, of whom there are many in the management hierarchy, who are the most important people because they actually provide the direct services to clients, which is the bread and butter of the Department — the reason for its existence in the first place. The less numerous but more generously paid senior level managers are also more dispensable, as demonstrated with the spilling of those positions that occurs every time there is a change of State Government. What do you think of that in relation to Melbourne Football Club?

JAMES McDONALD: Well … maybe we need a way to show that everybody is important. We have different roles to play but without lots of supporters we wouldn't have a club to play for — it just wouldn't be viable. And without reasonable players the supporters wouldn't have a team to barrack for. Without a strong club administration it couldn't all come together and the club wouldn't be able to participate in the AFL, and certainly wouldn't be competitive.

Me: Such old and wise words from a 'Junior'!

Chuckles.

Travis Johnstone: Yeah, I can see that the pointing-up pyramid isn't that helpful when talking to some young blokes in the team who might have pretty big heads as it is …

A few 'You'd know!' type comments and more chuckles.

Brad Green: There's probably a hierarchy amongst the players anyhow, but I don't think as a group we should be placed at the top of the club's tree any more than we should be placed at the bottom.

Me: You're not such a 'Greeny' for a youngster either. Another excellent point! And that's why I'd like to use this diagram …

As I draw on the whiteboard again.

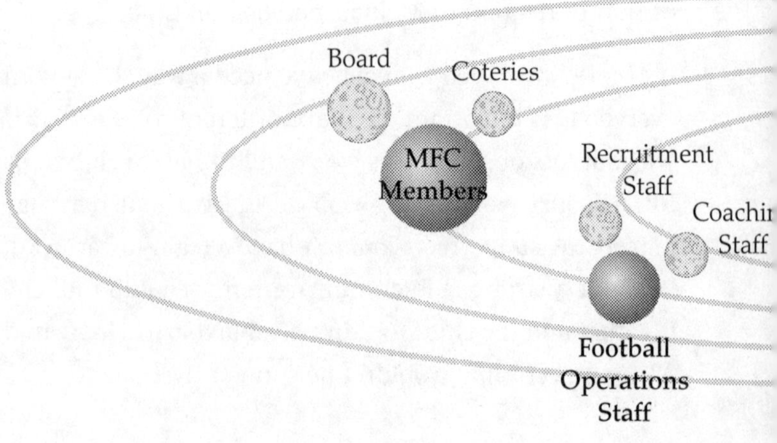

… which looks rather like a solar system, to represent where people and their different roles fit into the club. The sun in the middle represents one big star-team rather than a team of stars. The other groups making up the club, such as the coaching staff, sponsors, club administration, etcetera, orbit like planets around the sun as the solar system cycles through the football seasons.

Sub-groups, like the club's Board of Management, could be represented as a moon orbiting around a planet, which in turn might represent the club members.

The beauty of the solar system analogy is that, although depicted two-dimensionally here, if you think about it as a three-dimensional structure it represents each group as equal when you view it from the side … as if the solar system were a pancake. To take the analogy further, the MFC club structure can accommodate coming into contact, such as for matches, with other clubs in the AFL

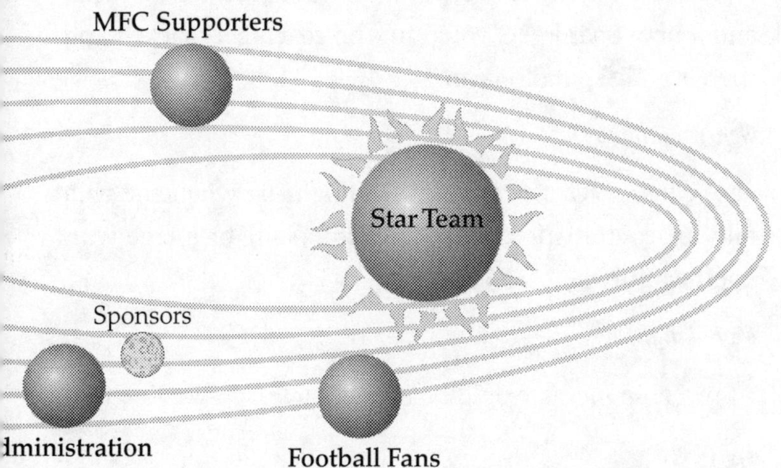

(which can be considered the universe) when the pancakes stack together like this. *I draw a series of horizontal lines, one under the other.*

Without stretching it too far, this analogy can also accommodate the notion that club structures and the overarching AFL are not static. There is movement of fans and supporters from year to year, probably not so much between clubs but within clubs as reflected in changing membership numbers. There is also movement of players into clubs (i.e. draft picks), between clubs (with trades and contracts not being renewed) and also out of clubs (such as retirements).

BEN BEAMS: Shooting stars, eh?

Chuckles and comments like, 'Shooting moonbeams, you mean!'

DAVID SCHWARZ: Yeah. You could have a comet representing a player going from one club to another, and a super nova representing when a team puts in a shocker of a season and a new Board gets voted in, the coach gets sacked and there's a big spill of players!

General laughter.

CAMERON BRUCE: Or the super nova might be when the club falls apart and is forced to move interstate or merge with another club.

More laughter.

ME: I reckon a merge would be a black hole.

Hysteria.

Just as I was working on my next one-liner, the thought struck me that it would be good to engineer someone to confirm the point that a solar system needs a degree of homeostasis or the orbiting planets may become erratic and collide. Then I could apply the analogy to the players and discuss the need for each individual within that stable yet flexible and evolving team structure to establish a balanced and thus relatively robust lifestyle — the very purpose of the session. I was nervous again, very tense. Too much to think about and too little time.

Potential material and exercises started racing through my head. Yes, we'd do one more exercise before taking a break. I'd get the boys to pair off again, maybe with different partners, and talk about their worst experiences. I don't like focusing on negative talk, but sometimes the illustration of a point through a less than ideal scenario helps to identify that positive actions are required to avoid falling into the same old traps and repeating situations.

I was suddenly concerned that such an exercise might induce tears and embarrass someone, or necessitate some debriefing or post-session counselling. I didn't want Neale to think I was trying to drum up business just because I'd waived my fee for this session. So I figured I'd better resume the next part of the session with a really positive exercise that exuded sharing and caring, tolerance of other people's differences, harmony and positive energy, helping each other, using each other's strengths and helping overcome their weaknesses, teamwork, maybe the role of mentoring ...

This was where I had started to wake up. The out of context noise and the sensation of the stiff neck were irrefutable evidence. With quite some effort I managed to recall most of the content of my dream as we journeyed along the Princes Highway. I even managed to jot down a few notes by the time we had arrived home. I thought it was pretty much off my mind by the time I went to bed, but strangely I had the same dream that very night! The same bumf came out of my mouth and the same diagrams were drawn on the same whiteboard with the same red and blue whiteboard markers, and it all elicited the same responses from the same players. How weird to have exactly the same dream — especially one with that level of detail — not once but twice in the one day! And so frustrating, too. I felt sure that I could have unlocked some more relevant, even revolutionary, material from the deepest, darkest recesses of my brain the second time around.

More importantly, I wondered *why* I had that dream? I'm by no means a dream analyst, but could it have been that I genuinely wanted to help my team work better together and ultimately bring success and glory to our great club again? Well, at a conscious level I certainly did want my team, in fact my entire club, to work better together and ultimately bring success and glory to MFC again (in my lifetime, please!). Particularly after the club's recent traumas; almost merging with Hawthorn at the end of 1997; and the MFC board elections looming with all the ingredients for a showdown between the faction headed by Joe Gutnick, the apparent financial saviour of the club at that dark hour in 1997, and the other group that included Robbie Flower.

But realistically, I doubted that I had anything of significance to contribute. Aside from continuing my club membership (continuous since season 1999), my attendance and support at Demons matches (all the home matches and increasingly more of the aways, as well), exercising my voting rights as a club member and encouraging other MFC members to do the same (both of which I did at the end of 2001, thereby helping the current Gabriel Szondy-led board into office), and trying to recruit more Melbourne Demons fans to join the club as members (I'm confident that I'll eventually wear down my friends, Jenny McAuley and Marg Downey, who are Melbourne Demons 'fans'). Mmmm. On second thoughts, I realised that I probably contributed quite a bit, really.

But there is usually something deeper and more subtle about the meaning of a dream, isn't there? What was this dream really trying to tell me? *Maybe that I wanted to be the centre of attention?* I doubt it. I hate the spotlight being on me, and it took me years to become comfortable getting up in front of colleagues as a training facilitator. *Maybe that I wanted to be a stand-up comedian?* Definitely not! I can be relied upon to stuff up the punch line of the (otherwise) funniest jokes. Best to leave humour to people like Marg, I think. *Maybe that the pre-season had come around too early for me in relation to my team?* Possibly. After all, the finals series had already started and Melbourne didn't make it that year. Perhaps the dream was just reinforcing how much footy was a part of my life — how important it was to me and that I didn't know how I'd cope until Season 2002 came around. But perhaps the detailed account of Patrick's arrival was to affirm that he is also a very important part of my life that cannot be forgotten even, or especially, when I am immersed in football. Ooh, what does that say about Bruce? (Well, he is a Collingwood supporter.) I wonder what the dream really meant. I just wonder.

Postscript I

And I was still pondering the meaning of my dream the next day, Tuesday, 11 September 2001. I was wandering aimlessly around Safeway at Kew, desperately trying to remember the items we needed (I had forgotten my shopping list again) just before midday when I chanced upon two old neighbours. Reg and his wife, Edna, were 'old neighbours' in both senses — they were elderly and they still lived in the house next door to our previous home where we had resided for ten years. We got talking, as you do, mainly with me responding to questions from them; How's Paddy? How's Bruce? How's the new house going? Then Edna asked what I thought about the events in America overnight.

'What events in America?' I asked. Edna and Reg did their best to bring me up to date with the terrorist attacks on the World Trade Center and the Pentagon. Edna told me she often had trouble sleeping and had been glued to the radio all night and then to the television all morning. Meanwhile I had gone to bed early the previous night and hadn't bothered to turn on the radio the next morning, still preoccupied with my strange dream. I had been totally absorbed in my own little world. How quickly my world changed that day.

Postscript II

My strange dream had been long gone from my mind, but a clue as to its real meaning seemed to present itself on the night 27 November 2001. I was at the MFC Members' Information Night when I had one of those 'aha' experiences.

There were plenty of players in attendance, including the

three new recruits — Clint Bizzell (from Geelong), Craig Ellis (from the Western Bulldogs) and Peter Vardy (from the Adelaide Crows) who were selected in the pre-draft trading. Jeff Farmer's recent decision to go to Fremantle was discussed in detail, particularly how it created opportunities for the club despite not having been the preferred option.

There was a big screen that showed footage from Season 2001 of the team playing and of the new boys playing with their previous clubs. There was nothing so unsophisticated as a whiteboard with red and blue markers in sight, but the background of most of the slides was red and blue. There were presentations by Tim Gaspar, Business Development Manager; Danny Corcoran, General Manager — Football Operations; Craig Cameron, Recruiting Manager; and Neale Daniher, Coach. I thought Neale's presentation was the best, just sensational. I've always been a big wrap for Neale (even if he did play for Essendon) and I reckon he's done a great job since coming to MFC. But at the Members' Information Night he was very impressive — very thorough, very considered yet also very spontaneous, very open to feedback, very enthusiastic, very motivating, very inspiring! I was not at all surprised to hear that it was Neale who initiated the inaugural MFC Members' Information Night in 1999. I could go on and on, but suffice it to say that I respect Neale even more since the night of 27 November 2001, and I now think of him as Coach to all the members of the club, not just to the players.

My 'aha' experience occurred, however, not during Neale's presentation but during Danny Corcoran's. Danny was talking about where the club was heading in the foreseeable future and he put up a slide to outline the vision established by the MFC Board, Administration and Football Department that year. The slide featured, wait for it, a pyramid! Okay, it was a triangle, but it represented a pyramid.

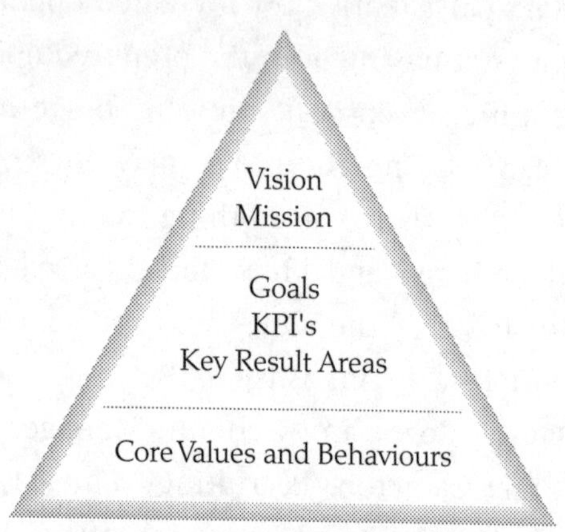

Oh, my excitement. I could barely contain myself. I still wasn't really sure what that dream of a few months prior meant, but I was beginning to wonder if I had simply projected my optimism and enthusiasm to ensure that my team used the 2002 pre-season better than ever before. Seeing for myself at the Members' Information Night the thoroughness of the pre-season planning and preparation, and the genuinely positive attitude being taken by the key people at MFC in moving forward into the next season, into the next several seasons in fact, was exactly what I had been hoping for. Yes, even dreaming of. I could see then that my 'dream' session with the players on maintaining a balance in their lives was totally superfluous. They had all been involved in the development of the club's core values and behaviours; to be trustworthy, committed, smart, organised, empathic and positive.

Equally encouraging and uplifting for me personally was the message reiterated in various ways by each of the speakers regarding the importance with which the club views the role of its members and supporters — the Penny Mackiesons of the world.

> *This is Melbourne! … The Melbourne Football Club comprises more than just the playing list and coaching staff. It doesn't stop with the administration or the property steward. Sponsors play an important part BUT our team is not even close to being complete without YOU — our members and supporters.*[10]

In fact, Danny Corcoran presented the mission of MFC: '… to give the members the opportunity to be part of something extraordinary.' I certainly felt like I was part of something extraordinary — an extraordinary dream, an extraordinary Members' Information Night, an extraordinary footy club. I was ready. I was ready for AFL Premiership Season 2002. Bring it on!

Rock it to Me, Demons!

Sunday, 24 February 2002, 10.17 a.m.
Email to Dawn

I'm loathe to read too much into the Demons' performance in the pre-season competition, though I am very glad that they played a lot better on Friday night than the previous week's effort, even if we didn't win. Michael Voss really stood up in the last quarter, having been quiet for most of the match. And what hypocrisy, David Neitz getting rubbed out for his misdemeanour of last week but Plugger getting off! Plugger's unduly rough play looked as deliberate as it could be to me! Oh well, nothing like a good old controversy to start the year.

Wednesday, 13 March 2002, 10.23 p.m.
Email from Dawn

What about the Wayne Carey story? Huge!

Saturday, 16 March 2002, 5.13 p.m.

Email to Dawn

Absolutely outrageous. And I bet there's a lot of AFL footballers out there who are glad it's him and not them, though. Probably a number who will be terminating their extra-marital relationships quick smart … Obviously it takes two people to tango and Kelli Stevens is equally responsible for what has happened. They both should have known better.

Wednesday, 27 March 2002, 5.16 p.m.

Email from Melbourne Football Club

… Meet the Directors & Past Players

Former club champions Garry Lyon, … Robert Flower, … and Greg Healy will be out in force on Monday from 12.30 p.m. outside Gate 6 (Punt Road end). Come and see the guys, say hi and collect their autographs …

Monday, 1 April 2002

MCG, Hawthorn versus Melbourne (Round 1)

Season 2002 was *finally* underway. Paddy and I had been hanging out for this *all* summer, even though Paddy got so anxious just before the game that he announced he didn't want to go. At the ground we soon spotted Robbie Flower, exchanging pleasantries with passing Demons supporters. Despite the butterflies in my stomach, I pulled out my No. 2 Demons guernsey (which I had packed just in case) and a black indelible marker pen (doesn't everybody carry one?) out of my backpack …

ME: Hi, Robbie. Congratulations on the Board elections last year.

RF: Thanks.

ME: (*Holding the guernsey and marker pen.*) Would you mind?

RF: Not at all. (*Holding the guernsey.*) It's my original colours!

ME: I've had this jumper for such a long time — I even used to fit into it. Now this one does. (*Pointing at six-year-old Patrick, clinging to my T-shirt from the safety of my back.*)

RF: Oh, give it a go! (*Chuckling good-humouredly. He signed the number '2' on the back of the jumper and returned it.*) Have a good day, now.

ME: You too.

The scores were close at the first break — we might have been just ahead. The second quarter was a fantastic display of football by the Demons, kicking some eight straight and unanswered goals. We were nearly 50 points up at half time, yet I dared not think the match was all over, worried that the Demons had already run out of legs on this hot April Fools' Day. The Demons kicked the first goal of the third quarter, but then the Hawks went up a gear and kicked ten goals straight. David Neitz had been great up forward in the first half, but was moved to the backline in an attempt to stem the flow. Then, close to where we were sitting, Neita got a corky (somewhere) after being sandwiched between two Hawks in a contest for the ball. He called for the trainer then for one of the medical staff, but stayed on the ground. Needless to say, Neita could not halt the run of opposition goals. And Travis Johnstone, who had been fantastic in the first half, made two terrible errors from kick-outs that resulted in a goal each time to Hawthorn.

> At three-quarter time we were
> a goal down. The Demons simply had to
> show some good old-fashioned
> ticker if they were to win.

Premature as it was, I felt like the character of the Demons' entire season was on the line in the fourth quarter.

The Hawks were much more highly fancied going into the match, but could the Demons stand up and take the victory they had earned in the first half? Neita started the final term on the bench — probably due to that corky. He was soon on the ground and up forward where he had been so effective in the first half. The first few minutes of play were an arm wrestle. Then Neita's decisive play turned the match — he attempted to mark but his opponent (all over him like a rash!) punched the ball from his grasp. A Hawk defender grabbed the ball, then Neita grabbed the defender in an iron-grip tackle and dumped him on the ground. The ball spilled free, was crumbed by one of our forwards and snapped through for a goal. I was now *very* confident that our boys *would* win, and that our 'captain courageous' had made the match-winning play that would inspire our boys on to victory.

Indeed, we won by 26 points. Neita kicked 5-2, while Travis Johnstone was probably best on ground, despite those two mistakes in the third term. We sang (all I had left was a squeak, really) several rounds of our club song and clapped our boys off the ground before heading home. We arrived in time to see the replay from midway though the third quarter, which we videotaped and replayed at least twice before Patrick's bedtime.

'Have a good day, now,' Robbie Flower, my all-time football hero, had said to me before the match. And that is exactly what I had! I met Robbie in person. I cheered my team on to win a rocking, rollercoaster of a match. My favourite player had a sensational game, leading from the front in courageous and emphatic style. My favourite boy had toughed out the anxieties of the day and revelled in our team's victory with me. It was only Round 1, but it doesn't get much better than that ... With the exception of winning a premiership, of course!

● WIN/LOSS RATIO 1:0 — ATTENDANCE 1:0

Sunday, 7 April 2002

MCG, Melbourne versus Port Adelaide (Round 2)

What a difference a week can make in football. The Demons played against another much more fancied side, Port Adelaide, the 2002 Wizard Home Loans Cup winners — in fact, back-to-back pre-season Cup winners. Last week Paddy was anxious and nervous about the match, even saying he didn't want to attend, both before and during the game. This week, as we were walking down from Wellington Parade after Bruce dropped us off just after 2.00 p.m., Paddy bolted for the entrance when he heard the Demons' club song come over the

MCG loudspeakers. He didn't even want to get hot chips before going to our seats — didn't want to miss the first bounce! We made it just in time.

A week can indeed make a big difference in football, but some things can be a bit déjà vu, too. For example, the Demons kicked towards the city end in the first quarter — again. We got off to a good start in the first, seemed to be going nowhere fast in the second and third quarters, but were still right in it at three-quarter time with the scores locked on 69 points apiece. The stage was set for the second time in a week for the Demons to stand up, show some ticker and take the game. Once again they would be kicking towards the end in which we were seated in the final quarter. I couldn't have written the script better myself, because that's exactly what happened. And David Neitz, my 'captain courageous', finished with another handy contribution to the scoreboard. Keep it coming, Dees!

● WIN/LOSS RATIO 2:0 — ATTENDANCE 2:0

Saturday, 13 April 2002

MCG, Richmond versus Melbourne (Round 3)

Paddy and I attended as visitors of a friend, Graeme Younger, to the MCC. Graeme, a Demons fan, doesn't go to the footy as much as he would like, as his boys aren't very keen. We sat on ground level in the Ponsford Stand towards the city end goals. The match went much like the previous two matches, with the exception that the umpiring seemed biased (towards the Tigers!). There were a number of soft decisions at crucial times. (I reckon that Tiger, Ben Holland, has got the hardest, most muscular and chiselled-looking body in the AFL — it could have been carved by Michelangelo. But he's as soft as a pair of fluffy slippers. Honestly! In two performances today, both worthy of Oscar nominations, Ben Holland played for and received a free kick, one of which resulted when the nearest body part of a Demons player was *at least* six inches away. Sucked in, umpie!)

Thank goodness the Richmond forwards weren't kicking too straight or they would have blown us away. The Demons didn't play especially well, but hung in there to be two points up at three-quarter time. The stage was set, for the third week in a row, for a tight, potentially heart-stopping, final quarter.

But this week it wasn't to be. The hardness at the ball that was there in the previous two final quarters was lacking in all but a few of the players, and the Tigers ran over us. Luckily Paddy wasn't too distressed. What with the novelty of sitting with Graeme, and in the Members', Paddy kept saying, 'It's a good view from here!' It wasn't really anywhere near as good a view as we would get from our regular seats, but it was different. Paddy busied himself recording the scores in the *AFL Record* when things got a bit too stressful for him.

● WIN/LOSS RATIO 2:1 — ATTENDANCE 3:0

Saturday, 20 April 2002

Optus Oval, Melbourne versus West Coast (Round 4)

The first 'home' match for Melbourne at Optus Oval. An interesting experiment, I suppose. I passed up a She Devils pre-match function because I thought it would be too difficult organising for Paddy to attend the match. But in the end, Paddy decided not to come at all (probably worried we'd lose given last week's result). I met a friend, Keri Whitehead, there anyway. She was coming with me to a concert in which my singing group was performing that evening, and was staying the night at our place.

I left home later than I'd planned and made the mistake of going via the Eastern Freeway — got stuck in footy traffic for the G as well as for Optus. By the time I got to the ground, the first car park was full, so I went on to the next. A few frantic mobile phone calls with Keri and we eventually met up. By the time we sat down the match was well underway, with the score 14 points apiece. Basically, from that point on, the Demons started kicking away from the West Coast Eagles and didn't let up. Neita was holding his marks and converting them, and Brad Green was exciting. Clint Bizzell was solid in defence, as was Craig Ellis, who made his debut for Melbourne today.

The match was good viewing for Melbourne supporters; barely a 'Weagles' fan in sight. The crowd looked a reasonable size to me, possibly 15,000–20,000, so I was shocked to hear the official crowd figure — just over 9,300. The small size of the stadium clearly deceived me. Anyway, I was in heaven. The Demons were playing consistent footy, not letting up on their opposition, keeping at the scoreboard and not just pro-tecting a lead. It's official. I feel comfortable now in saying that it's a good start to the season by the Dees.

● WIN/LOSS RATIO 3:1 — ATTENDANCE 4:0

Friday, 26 April 2002

Colonial Stadium, Western Bulldogs versus Melbourne (Round 5)

I had not planned to attend this match (I'm usually pretty tired on a Friday night), rather to prop in front of the telly with Paddy and some crisps (and maybe a Ruskie or two, too!). I picked Paddy up from After School Care at about 6 p.m., organised a pizza from the shop over the road, and turned on the telly in readiness. Turned it on all right, but the reception was shot. (Shit!) I fiddled with the joins of the temporary extension leads we have been using for the aerial connection while our renovations are in progress — no improvement. I checked the back of the TV where the aerial lead plugs in — decidedly saggy looking. Gave it a bit of a wiggle and the (bloody!) thing broke off in my hand (me, Tarzan?). The reception was totally shot now.

The only option at a few minutes notice was a little TV, combined with radio and CD player, that I had bought a couple of years ago.

> Our regular TV has a 64 cm screen —
> the alternative, a 15 cm screen.
> But when you're desperate,
> anything will do.

So there we were, having pulled our dining chairs up to within two feet of the big telly, on which the mini-TV had been placed. Bruce tuned it through the VCR, so at least the reception was decent. Whenever the camera panned back to show a full shot of the ground, we leaned forward in unison in order to make out the teams, let alone the individual players.

The Bulldogs dominated play in the first quarter, but were embarrassingly inaccurate and led by only two points at the first break. The Demons started to get going in the second term, and eventually ran out winners by 23 points. Shane Woewodin found form — according to Garry Lyon, it was possibly his best performance since winning the Brownlow Medal in 2000. Neitz was, once again, also fantastic. He kicked three goals and, to quote Eddie McGuire, was involved in at least four assists on other Demons goals. I think it was Eddie who also commented that Neita may be 'the most inspirational skipper of the season so far'.

I'm almost convinced that Melbourne's performance against Richmond in Round 3 was an anomaly; they have finished off every other match strongly in the fourth quarter. Couldn't quite convince Graeme Younger of that at Auskick the next day, but promised to persevere the following week.

● WIN/LOSS RATIO 4:1 — ATTENDANCE 4:1

Tuesday, 30 April 2002

I got home from work to find a message on the answering machine from John Anderson, CEO of MFC, to advise that I had won second prize in the MFC Members Only raffle. Second prize being a trip for two (airfares, transfers and accommodation) for six days *to Thailand!*

Sunday, 5 May 2002

SCG, Sydney versus Melbourne (Round 6)

I watched Channel Nine's coverage live on the telly. The Dees were certainly lacklustre in the first quarter, didn't score a goal. But they looked to be on the comeback trail in the following two quarters. Still, it's no good letting the opposition jump out of the blocks — catch-up footy is not the way to win a premiership! Neita didn't play his best game, either — only two goals. The marks just weren't sticking. The feature article in the *Herald Sun* today probably put the mocker on him. And just when things seemed to be going so well!

- WIN/LOSS RATIO 4:2 — ATTENDANCE 4:2

Tuesday, 14 May 2002

Email to Sinead Wise

> *I was hoping for a good old-fashioned shellacking by our boys against the Saints on Sunday as a bonus Mother's Day gift. I was there, along with my reason for being a mum, and I said to Paddy about half way through the first quarter, 'I'll be happy if we can just take away the four points, never mind the percentage!' The Dees really didn't play very well, but good enough to win, eh? We really missed Powelly and Bizz, but the Ox was sensational.*

- WIN/LOSS RATIO 5:2 — ATTENDANCE 5:2

Sunday, 19 May 2002

Email to Dawn

> *Bet you are rapt with the Pies' big win over the Lions last night. It was a terrific game, had everything. Tarrant and Bucks were*

just on fire, and what about Rupe bobbing up at the crucial time and turning the match? I wish the same could be said for the Dees. Fancy the Wizard winning the match for the Dockers after the siren. Cheeky little bugger, and after he goaled from a dubious free kick only minutes prior. Honestly.

- WIN/LOSS RATIO 5:3 — ATTENDANCE 5:3

Saturday, 25 May 2002

MCG, Melbourne versus Kangaroos (Round 9)

I watched this match from the second level of the Members' Stand, as a guest of an old college friend, Terry Jasper. He is a Kangaroos supporter, as are his parents who were down from Rutherglen for the match. The match was a pretty tight and tense affair. I was quite distracted, what with having a good natter to Terry for most of the time, but was pretty relieved by the Demons' narrow win (to be honest, I thought a bit of luck went our way with the umpiring). I tried (pretended!) not to look too pleased out of deference to the many Kangaroos supporters surrounding me.

- WIN/LOSS RATIO 6:3 — ATTENDANCE 6:3

Saturday, 1 June 2002

Baytec Stadium, Geelong versus Melbourne (Round 10)

There was no way I was ever going to attend this match, and no way Melbourne was ever going to win it (not that the two things are at all related). The Demons haven't won at Geelong since 1988! And I've gotten over my superstition of a few years ago that the Demons would only win if I went to the match, just in case you were wondering!

- WIN/LOSS RATIO 6:4 — ATTENDANCE 6:4

Monday, 10 June 2002

MCG, Melbourne versus Collingwood (Round 11)

I attended this match with Dawn and some other friends of hers. As things turned out, it was a very masochistic thing to do. Lunch at the AFL Members' bistro was the highlight of my afternoon. I am currently feeling decidedly anxious about how the Demons' season is progressing. It's not good when you're halfway into the season and your personal attendance record exceeds your team's win/loss ratio!

- WIN/LOSS RATIO 6:5 — ATTENDANCE 7:4

Saturday, 22 June 2002

Optus Oval, Melbourne versus Adelaide (Split Round 12)

Paddy and I attended the Demons' second home game at Optus. Bloody ridiculous idea. Spent twenty minutes stuck in traffic in Royal Parade — took forty-five minutes to get there from Kew, for goodness sake! The match had been underway about three to four minutes by the time we got to our reserved seating area. Plenty of room, at least. A larger crowd than against the Eagles, but still not flash (approximately 12,000). I thoroughly understand why Melbourne supporters don't like going there!

But I soon forgot my frustration. Melbourne played a good solid first quarter of footy, but was still down at quarter time.

They came out firing in the second quarter and soon earned the lead, from which point they were never headed. Our boys won by 25 points — a well deserved victory through four consistent quarters of footy. The best I have seen the Demons play all year — contributors all over the ground, including Yze, Woey, Johnno, Neita, Greeny, Brucey, etc. Good to see Neita kick three goals, though he would have bagged five had he kicked straight. Never mind, he was winning the ball!

Whatever their motivation, it was a key match for our boys. After our defeat by the Magpies only a few weeks ago, I thought they were just going to loll back to the middle of the pack. But now, *if they can just keep it going*, I think the Dees can be contenders. All the more important that we get plenty of supporters to our next match against the Bombers at *their* home ground next week!

● WIN/LOSS RATIO 7:5 — ATTENDANCE 8:4

Friday, 28 June 2002

*Colonial Stadium, Essendon versus Melbourne
(Round 13)*

I can tell you right now that I will *never again* book a ticket for a Melbourne away game at Colonial Stadium via the automated phone system! I'm glad it was a night match and I didn't even consider taking Paddy along. I ended up sitting among Essendon Football Club members in a seat resold because the respective member whose reserved seat it was decided not to attend the match! And Colonial touts this as 'best available' seating on Level 2 — well *not* for away team supporters, *you idiots!* I had to put up with three women sitting directly behind me who screamed throughout the match, 'You animal!', at David Schwarz *every* time he went anywhere near the ball. In the first quarter, Schwarz had been involved in a hip and shoulder incident, deemed by the umpire to be a bit late, on an Essendon player — *but he was only a second late compared with the five minute delay involved in the hip and shoulder Michael Long put on Melbourne's Troy Simmonds in the 2000 Grand Final!* (Some Essendon supporters, at least, must have very short memories!) As if that wasn't bad enough, the three Bomber witches also screeched, 'You moron!', *every* time any other Melbourne player went near the ball. I really don't know why they bothered; they clearly don't know the meaning of the word or they wouldn't have drawn such attention to themselves!

● WIN/LOSS RATIO 7:6 — ATTENDANCE 9:4

Thursday, 4 July 2002, 3.24 p.m.
Email from Sinead Wise

> *I am devastated. I've just heard the news that The Ox is retiring. I just don't know what to say.*

My subsequent thought, which I figured was best kept to myself as David Schwarz was Sinead's favourite player, was that those three Bomber witches cast a nasty spell on him!

Wednesday, 10 July 2002, 5.49 p.m.
Email to Sinead Wise

> *It certainly was a shock, wasn't it? I thought he was playing pretty good footy, too, this year — hard to believe he has run out*

of fire in his belly ... My eyes filled with tears when he came on The Footy Show and, for once, I thought Sam Newman treated him with due respect for the champion he is. (Yes, I have been watching The Footy Show a bit lately. I still haven't forgiven Newman for the pie incident, but I reckon he has toned down somewhat since then.)

Just changing the subject for a moment, wasn't it a great win by the boys at the Gabba on the weekend?! I was so proud of them, and absolutely glued to the telly. Didn't Neita give Mal Michael and Leppitsch a bath?! That's my boy!

● WIN/LOSS RATIO 8:6 — ATTENDANCE 9:5

Sunday, 14 July 2002

Colonial Stadium, Carlton versus Melbourne (Round 15)

It was with great trepidation that I got on the Ticketmaster7 website to book Paddy's ticket and mine for this match. I had decided that Level 1 was the safest spot (couldn't trust Colonial to sell decent tickets on Level 2!), and almost couldn't believe the great seats we got; third row from the fence, and two seats in from the aisle that the Melbourne coaching staff used to access the coaching box! Paddy and I were so close to Neale Daniher that we could see the smug grin on his face getting bigger and bigger at the end of each quarter. 'Onya, Neale!' I yelled whenever he went past. Neita looked the most relaxed and confident I've ever seen him play — he kicked nine goals! A most memorable shellacking of the Blues that most cer-tainly took the gloss off Koutoufides' return!

● WIN/LOSS RATIO 9:6 — ATTENDANCE 10:5

Saturday, 20 July 2002

MCG, Melbourne versus Hawthorn (Round 16)

We missed Melbourne's '1000 @ "our" MCG' match because this was the only time we were able to book our holiday to Thailand. Bruce and I were the recipients of the prize, while we paid extra for Paddy to come, too. After all, Paddy is a Melbourne Football Club member and it wouldn't have been right for a Collingwood fan to take his place on a trip that only came about through Paddy and me being MFC members! We logged onto the Internet after the match, though, only to be disappointed by the result. (Maybe it would have made a difference if we had been there, supporting the boys!)

- WIN/LOSS RATIO 9:7 — ATTENDANCE 10:6

Saturday, 27 July 2002

Football Park, Port Adelaide versus Melbourne (Round 17)

Annoyed that yet another of Melbourne's interstate matches was not televised by Channel Ten. Had to follow the match on the radio — again!

- WIN/LOSS RATIO 9:8 — ATTENDANCE 10:7

Sunday, 4 August 2002

MCG, Melbourne versus Richmond (Round 18)

The high point of the day was Neita's five goals — he still leads the goal-kicking ladder. The mercurial Robbo also kicked five. But it just wasn't enough. Oh, the worry of it all!

- WIN/LOSS RATIO 9:9 — ATTENDANCE 11:7

Sunday, 11 August 2002
Subiaco, West Coast versus Melbourne (Round 19)

Why won't they telecast Melbourne's interstate matches? It's just not fair! (Bruce won't let Paddy and I get pay TV — he says we watch enough footy as it is!)

● WIN/LOSS RATIO 10:9 — ATTENDANCE 11:8

Sunday, 18 August 2002
MCG, Melbourne versus Western Bulldogs (Round 20)

Neita celebrated his 200th game today by kicking seven more goals. Paddy and I were very proud to see this one live. It was a good tussle, which our boys won by 12 points. But on the downside, Ellis did his knee, right in front of us, about four minutes into the first term. Not a good turn of events for our back line, having lost Alistair Nicholson early in the season and Troy Broadbridge later through knee injuries. But the Demons are still in with a good chance of seeing finals action. Oooh, it's tight!

● WIN/LOSS RATIO 11:9 — ATTENDANCE 12:8

Saturday, 24 August 2002
MCG, Melbourne versus Sydney (Round 21)

I would love to have been there, cheering the boys on, but months ago we planned to go skiing this weekend at Mount Hotham with a group of people from Bruce's work. (Tisk, tisk — typical MFC supporter behaviour, eh?) Bruce and I hadn't been skiing for more than ten years, and Paddy had never been before. I was excited to be doing it again after all these years, but I didn't want to get too tired or stiff (particularly as I've had knee surgery since the last time I went skiing, and hadn't done any training for this trip). So I came in from the slopes and was seated with a chardonnay in time for the commencement of the second quarter. I didn't exactly drown my sorrows, rather I found two congenial skiers to chat with while the Swans set about shellacking the Demons. (Bugger!) Can the boys still make it into the finals? It's going to be a *very* close thing.

● WIN/LOSS RATIO 11:10 — ATTENDANCE 12:9

Saturday, 31 August 2002

Colonial Stadium, St Kilda versus Melbourne (Round 22)

Oh, the stress of it all! I felt that Melbourne absolutely had to win this match to ensure not only a place in the final eight, but to develop some momentum and give ourselves any chance of winning a finals match. There was no way I was taking Paddy to this one: Firstly, I would have had to remain unstressed (fat chance!) so that I could work effectively on minimising his stress (he generates enough for both of us at the best of times!). Secondly, it was a night match and I had never taken him to one before. Finally, it was a Saints home game, so there was sure to be lots of rowdy (among other things) Saints supporters in attendance. I took Bruce instead; Paddy stayed over at Bruce's parents'. Once again I managed to book great seats via the Internet — we were several rows from the fence, but very close to the Demons' race. Bruce will tell you I was so stressed throughout the match that I barely sat in my seat, jumping up and down every time the ball came down our end, or when there was a close umpiring decision. (That may or may not be true.) But I was only truly convinced we would win the match with about five minutes to go, when young Steven Armstrong bobbed up with two exciting goals in as many minutes. The overwhelming feeling at the end of the match was relief, pure and simple! We had made it to the finals, after all. So much for our great start to the season — all that mattered now was the result of our *next* match.

 • WIN/LOSS RATIO 12:10 — ATTENDANCE 13:9

Sunday, 8 September 2002
MCG, Melbourne versus Kangaroos
(Elimination Final)

Back at our home, the G, Paddy and I were most comfortable. The Kangaroos never looked like heading our boys. I probably should have been feeling stressed, given it was an *elimination* match for our team, but I always felt confident, both in the lead-up to and during this one. I guess I felt that the Kangaroos had used up more than their fair share of talent and nervous energy during the season to make it into the final eight — they had shown incredible courage to plough on after the loss of Carey through less than auspicious circumstances before the season had even got going, but I reckoned the players couldn't ride on that wave of emotion forever. The match was more about the Kangaroos running out of puff than about what the Demons had to do to win, as far as I was concerned.

And I wasn't disappointed, not the least because my boy Neitz gave Mick Martin an absolute bath (in fact, Neita made Martin look even older, slower *and* uglier than usual)! Oh, it was getting very hard to control my excitement! The Demons might not have looked so great heading into the finals, but once in, it's their current form that matters. Go Dees!

● WIN/LOSS RATIO 13:10 — ATTENDANCE 14:9

Saturday, 14 September 2002
MCG, Melbourne versus Adelaide
(Semi-Final)

Following on from the previous week's performance, I was feeling good; so good and confident about Melbourne's chances of winning this semi-final match that I braved it to take Paddy for his first ever night match (well, I braved it by taking Bruce along, too — moral support for us both).

The Dees were, however, off to one of their ridiculously bad starts. Forty points down at quarter time. This felt very déjà vu. I couldn't help but remember my thoughts when the rot started (Round 6 against Sydney) … letting the opposition jump out of the blocks is so obviously *not* the way to win a premiership (especially against the Crows who have tasted two in recent years)! Poor wee Paddy! He grizzled all the way through the first quarter that the match was '… too one-sided! I want to go home!' Of course, we wouldn't let him. We both have an aversion to bringing up a child to think you should just cut your losses when the going gets a little bit tough. I kept telling Paddy, 'Don't worry, mate. The Dees will fight their way back, and they always come home strong in the final term.' In fact, this had been a real strength of the Demons throughout the season (right from the outset!), even in matches that they had ended up losing.

And the Demons *did* fight their way back, magnificently, during the second and third quarters — real good, solid footy, like they played to beat the Brisbane Lions at the Gabba in Round 14 after giving away a huge lead in the first quarter (could they do it again?). In fact, we were up by a couple of kicks at three-quarter time.

The stage was set for another final quarter showdown; a battle to determine if the Demons had the ticker to stand up and finish off the job ... *if they could just keep it going!* More déjà vu that I could have done without. Way too much déjà vu! (Talk about stress — it doesn't get much worse than this!)

Mirroring how the Demons' season had started with the Round 1 clash against Hawthorn, the character of the Demons' entire season was once again on the line in the fourth quarter. But this time there would be no next week to redeem themselves if they didn't make it; this time it was all or nothing. I was all too mindful that Melbourne hadn't strung more than two wins together *all* season — they had won their Round 22 match, then the Elimination Final last week, and ... they were not due for a win this week on their season's form. They would have to break a very strong pattern, against all the odds, if they were to stay in the running for the 2002 Premiership!

Five minutes into the final term it was evident that the Demons had nothing left in the fuel tank. The exertion of fighting their way back into the match after the first-quarter drubbing had obviously taken its toll. David Neitz was doing his best to motivate and encourage his charges, but even 'captain courageous' was unable to make a play sufficiently inspirational to lift the boys above their exhaustion. I looked across at Bruce and said, 'We've run out of legs!' The Demons were progressively run over during the quarter — they had all but come to a standstill.

The situation was grim but, as usual, there were some lighter moments that I expect to savour (cling to?) for a while. For example, the man who, in fine (possibly somewhat ale-assisted) form yelled out, 'Go, Brownlow!', every time Shane Woewodin went near the ball. The name might not have been original, but it was clear to all within earshot whom the spectator was referring to, and the high esteem in which he held the player. The same witty spectator also yelled, 'Go, Silk!', every time Travis Johnstone had possession. The keen Melbourne Demons fan was obviously in awe of the boy's *silky* football skills. Paddy and I usually just call young Johnno, 'What A Mess', after the cartoon named in honour of the dishevelled Afghan pup that is the star of the show (you'll know what we mean if you care to take a look at Johnno's hairdo), so we really giggled every time the spectator called him 'Silk'.

The funniest comment we (well I, at least) heard was a little more complex to explain to the seven year old present. Quite possibly the same funny, and progressively inebriated, man (there's a clown in every crowd, isn't there?) took it upon himself during a particularly low patch for Demons supporters in the final quarter to explain to nearby Crows supporters what a fine thing their club had done in securing the 'services' (wink, wink, nod, nod!) of Wayne Carey for the next year. He said something along the lines that it was positively magnanimous of the Crows players to come all the way over to Victoria this evening so as to afford their wives and girlfriends an unfettered opportunity to give Carey a 'real welcome' (wink, wink, nod, nod!) to their club and city in their absences. I snickered out loud, which I shouldn't have, because the inevitable questions followed: 'Mum, what are Wayne Carey's *services*?' and 'Mum, what did the man mean when he said "a *real* welcome"?'

But poor, poor little Paddy! He wasn't distracted for long. He literally buried his head in my jumper and cried every time the Crows scored a goal, and his sobbing was relentless during the last ten minutes of the match. I felt cruel for making him sit through it (especially as the Crows are not among my favourite teams), but we scampered as soon as the loudspeakers struck up, 'We're the pride of South Oz-stray-lee-yah ...' Paddy stopped crying as soon as we left our seats (just as he did the day of the 2000 Grand Final when he became distraught after the RAAF Hornet flew over the stadium), and was in quite a good humour as we walked back to where we had parked our car in Victoria Parade. Paddy waved his Demons flag and kept saying, 'The Demons did well to get to the finals, didn't they Mum?'

Of course they did. And didn't David Neitz do well, too, giving us something extra special to savour from Season 2002 in the form of his Coleman Medal win — our club's first since the League's leading goal kicker award was introduced in 1955. Rock it to me, Neita! And rock it to me, Demons! I'd probably prefer it if the ride was a bit less rocky, but there's always next year for another tilt at the Premiership, eh?!

● WIN/LOSS RATIO 13:11 — ATTENDANCE 15:9

Learning to Believe

A Collingwood Supporter's Journey Through 2002

Sunday, 29 September 2002

Collingwood 9.12.66 lost to Brisbane 10.15.75

I've just woken up and wish that I hadn't. My first thought is my last thought: 'Why? How? How could we have lost it? Bloody Brisbane! Bloody goal umpires!' Can't sleep any more so get up and make tea. Flick on the television and what's on — another replay. Watched it — same ending though!

I don't think I've cried so much in a long time, not over football anyway. It was so heartbreakingly close all day. So close that the last fourteen hours have been full of 'if onlys'. If only Tarrant hadn't kicked into the man on the mark. If only Michael Voss was wearing black and white and not the other mob's colours. If only the goal umpire had seen what 90,000 other people saw; that Pebbles' shot went through the middle two sticks and was, therefore, a goal.

I think it was the sight of Mick in tears that finished me

off yesterday. You expect the boys to be upset. In the main they're young, they gave everything in the contest and they're not experienced in losing or winning big ones. But Mick — the steely-eyed, hard-headed veteran of umpteen finals series — who has won two, but lost one already, to see him openly weeping as he tried to console his charges. Well, then you knew how much this one hurt. Then at the press conference, 'But if I could pinch ten points from somewhere … I'd give my right leg for the ten points, but it's not to be.' He has only been at Collingwood for three years, but he's already one of the great Magpie men, and we will win a flag with him. I'm as sure of that as I've been of anything. What a season it's been though! Who would have thought we'd come so far …

Wednesday, 27 March 2002

Pre-season Matches: Lost 3, Won 1 (against St Kilda so it hardly counts!)

Woo hoo! Nearly the start of the footy season at last! Of course you don't count the pre-season games. They don't mean anything at all; they're the equivalent of the pre-game warm up, aren't they? To be fair, the losses to Sydney, Hawthorn and the Kangaroos were fairly disheartening but there were a couple of highlights — Cummings' bag of five against the Hawks for example — and it's good to see Damien Adkins looking so fit! Anyway, we know Mick's not a big fan of the pre-season so it's obvious he's setting the boys for a big start to the real stuff!

We have to make the Eight this year. Another year of 'nearly' won't be good enough. Last year was heart-breaking when we missed out by one lousy game, especially when you think about the ones that got away. Tell me, how often does Bucks kick five behinds in a game? Not often, I can tell you. But we lost that game by four points and that cost us the finals! No, calm down Dawn. It's another year and another chance. Everyone reckons we'll be in the finals — of course I have nagging doubts because there have been too many 'next years' since the last time.

The pre-season seems to be full of off-field drama with no story being bigger than the great Wayne Carey scandal. As Penny said to me, I'm sure there are a lot of other footballers who are looking at the events and saying, 'There but for the grace of God go I!' or words to that effect.

I'm starting the season with a gripe with the AFL and the way they treat us members. The latest iniquity involves the dining room. For years now, AFL members have been able to book into the Haydn Bunton Dining Room in the Southern Stand of the MCG for a meal before the game. The price of the meal also included a reserved seat, under cover in a prime spot in the Southern Stand. It's a great deal and a favourite of mine and my friends. This season, for no logical reason other than getting more money out of members, the AFL has decreed that we be charged $5.50 if we want a seat. Well, of course we want a seat! Can you imagine enjoying your lunch and then having to rush out a few minutes before game time to find a suitable spot? I guess I'll still go to the dining room but I'm not happy about it! I wonder what impact this will have on patronage.

It won't get much bigger as a start — Collingwood and Richmond on Easter Thursday night at the MCG! I've bribed, I mean persuaded, Hugh to come with me — he's been practising Matthew Richardson taunts for a few days now — and we're all set to go! The Tigers fans are full of it (well it rhymes with 'it' anyway!) about how close their boys got to the big one last year, and how this is their year — I just smile!

Thursday, 28 March 2002, 11.30 p.m.
Collingwood 18.10.118 lost to Richmond 24.11.155

That wasn't exactly in the script! Collingwood have just been smacked by the Tigers in front of a huge crowd. Richmond got off to a great start kicking nine goals in the first quarter against our four and it didn't get much better than that. Bloody Matthew 'pretty boy' Richardson had a field day and kicked six goals — where is the fun when he plays well, I ask? I got so pissed off we left at half time. I don't know what was worse, watching what was unfolding or listening to Hugh's commentary. I was tired and cranky and decided to beat the crowd home. Things were fairly even after quarter time but by then the damage was done. There were some good signs; Bucks looked in great touch and Scotty Cummings scored five goals — surely a contender for another Coleman Medal! Ah well, roll on the Eagles next week. We flogged them last year and should redeem ourselves against them at the G.

Saturday, 6 April 2002, 8.00 p.m.
Collingwood 17.18.120
defeated (just) West Coast 18.11.119

Phew that was close! There's something gone awry about this season. We should have won this one with one armed tied behind our backs but instead just scraped in as a result of a career-best performance by Brodie Holland — yes, I know it sounds bizarre!

I also got the answer to the dining room question. Would you believe the Bunton Room had to be closed and we were all shipped to the Carvery? As Ros, the lovely lady who looks after the dining room, said to me, 'Can you remember us not having the room open for a Collingwood game?' I signed a petition but I'm not confident — still, we'll wait and see.

Friday, 12 April 2002, 11.00 p.m.
Collingwood 7.13.55 lost to Carlton 11.9.75

Well it can't get much worse than this, can it? Losing to Carlton of all people. Same number of scoring shots and a 20 point deficit. Someone needs to point the forwards at the goals.

What I'm really mad about is the feral Carlton supporter who sat behind us and spat at us all night. I don't mind supporting your team but this one was foul-mouthed and totally obsessed with Nathan Buckley and his sexual habits! Penny and Keri heroically held me down or I'd have snotted the #%!*!

This is not the start of season I was looking for. The only consolation is that at least Carlton are a serious side — it's not like losing to a bottom team like West Coast!

Saturday, 20 April 2002, 10.30 p.m. (Sydney)
Collingwood 15.14.104 crush Hawthorn 9.9.63

Our first decent win for the year and I'm in Sydney. It's enough to cheese you right out of going to the football. I go to the first three games for two losses and a one-point win, I get sent to Sydney for work and the boys flog the Hawks! Of all the places to be, Sydney has to be the most frustrating! Footy is a two minute item on the evening news unless the Swans are involved, in which case it gets three minutes! Thankfully I had Internet access in Sydney so I could follow the game online, and hopefully Hugh has taped the replay. The important thing is that we won and won well. I've said before I'd never go to another game if I could be sure it meant a Magpies win. Honestly!

Now, hopefully, I'll be back in Melbourne in time for Anzac Day. Bring on the Bombers!

Thursday, 25 April 2002 (Anzac Day)
Collingwood 9.12.66 defeated Essendon 4.9.33

Well, as a famous former prime minister once said, 'This was the sweetest victory of all!' Until we win another flag!

Realising it was going to be a genuine blockbuster (and aren't these games always so?), I booked seats for myself and three like-minded friends as well as booking in for lunch. I took two Collingwood supporters; Tracey, who has shared so many highs and lows with me; Alison, who is a newer football companion but a passionate one nonetheless; and my mum, who is learning to be a Collingwood supporter. It's been a shocking day weather wise — absolutely pouring down — so we were lucky to have seats under cover. Logic says that I should have relaxed by three-quarter time, but I'm not very good at that. All around me, people were saying we had it won, and I kept maintaining that I wasn't sure. As one bloke behind me said, 'I'd hate to see you when it's close!' Given we were five goals up at that point and Essendon had only kicked two goals for the game, I guess he had a point.

It was a real wet weather game too — low scoring, lots of fumbles and mistakes and close, hard checking. There's no doubt, if Mick's taught the boys anything, he's taught them accountability. And, who's this kid McGough? How good is *he*? Winner of the Anzac Medal in his second game! Bruce Ruxton nearly burst his buttons with pride when he presented it! Mind you, I reckon Scotty Burns was stiff!

Saturday, 4 May 2002, 10.00 a.m.
Collingwood 16.15.111 flogged St Kilda 3.10.28

I didn't get to this match. I have to ration night games and make sure I get to ones I really want to see. As this was on television, I thought I'd pass.

All the talk last week was about 'the flood' and how Collingwood were going to beat it. St Kilda and Sydney had played a 'thrilling' draw last Saturday night, both employing flooding tactics. During the preview, Garry Lyon and Eddie talked about the Saints' tactics. They showed vision of last week's match where 36 players occupied less than a quarter of the ground. How will Collingwood combat it?, they said. 'Give it to Rocca and kick over the flood', I yelled at the television.

At the end of the day, it wasn't quite that simple but the principle was there. Collingwood played their own game and after the first half of the first quarter, when the Saints seemed to be dictating terms, things went pretty well. Nick Davis' four goals were good to see (three of them were in a ten minute burst in the second quarter) — shows how dangerous he can be. Only worry is Bucks being reported. I don't think he's got anything to worry about and it sounds like Andrew Thompson will be supportive. A nice little win all round!

Sunday, 12 May 2002

Collingwood 11.7.73
fluked it over Western Bulldogs 8.15.63

I missed this one because it was Mother's Day and I couldn't find a way to convince Mum that the ultimate treat for her was to go along to Colonial and watch the Magpies play. Instead, I took her out to lunch along with my best friend, Keri, and her mum, Jo. It was a very nice lunch and, best of all, we got home in time to watch the replay on Foxtel! Oops, sorry Mum! I'm glad I knew the result before I watched it as I could have been nervous otherwise. I have to be brutally honest and say that we didn't really deserve to win this one — but we'll take it because there will be other games that we will deserve to win and won't!

Saturday, 18 May 2002

Collingwood 17.12.114 defeated Brisbane 16.15.111

I'm sorry. I'll just say that again.
Collingwood defeated Brisbane!

I know, that's indulgent, but it was pretty good and is still a bit hard to believe.

I really meant to go to this match but somehow I didn't.

Maybe because I'm going to Adelaide next week and didn't want to push things — I don't know. Anyway, I didn't get there. It was on delayed telecast on TV and I was all set to do my usual — you know, radio in one ear, TV in the other — when Hugh stepped in and confiscated the radio. 'Why don't you watch it as though it's a live game?' he said.

'Why would I want to do that?' I replied.

'It'll be more fun!' was his response.

I wasn't convinced but decided to play along. I didn't have much choice seeing as he'd hidden my radio! What a nail-biter it was too! First Brisbane got away, then Collingwood pegged back before hitting the front thanks to a Rupert (Rupe! Rupe!) Betheras goal in the third quarter. The last quarter was a classic arm wrestle where the Bears (I mean the Lions) threw everything at my boys! I was marching up and down, yelling at the television, yelling at Hugh, drinking wine, willing them over the line! Oh the relief when the siren sounded! I don't think the neighbours could have coped with another ten minutes of that.

So, the state of play is: Collingwood are 6–2 after eight rounds and are equal top of the ladder. Next week we take on the Port Adelaide boys in another 'top of the ladder clash' and I'll be there!

Friday, 24 May 2002 (Adelaide)

Collingwood 12.14.86 have been pipped at the post by Port Adelaide 14.7.91

I want to go home! No, I want the world to open up and swallow me whole! I want the Collingwood forward line to have kicking lessons again! I want to be anywhere but Adelaide right this moment.

I don't want to talk about it. Suffice to say, Pebbles missed a shot that he should have got (actually he may have got but who'd trust South Australian umpires?) that would have tied the game. Instead we lost! And I'm never going to Football Park again!

Sunday, 2 June 2002

Collingwood 14.11.95 defeated Sydney 12.12.84

It's Hugh's birthday today and we've had a house full of guests for dinner (well, three people anyway). Like Mum on Mother's Day, I couldn't persuade Hugh that a trip to the footy was the way to celebrate, so I cooked dinner instead and found lots of excuses to run to the radio and TV to check the progress. I had a few nervous moments in the second and third terms and there were stages when my guests were concerned about the progress of their dessert, but fortunately for all, Collingwood ran out winners and kept their position on the ladder.

Monday, 10 June 2002

Collingwood 19.12.126 defeated Melbourne 10.15.75

Well, this was a tricky one. On the one hand, I'm thrilled that the boys have recorded such a convincing win over such quality opposition. On the other, I'm afraid Penny will never speak to me again.

I went to the match with Penny as usual, only this year we were joined by some friends; namely Keri (neutral but providing moral support to Penny), Stuart (definitely Collingwood) and Jean Marc (not sure he understands football at all!). We went to lunch in the dining room and had fantastic seats on centre wing — everything you could want, really. And the match was everything I could want. After Melbourne had the first five scoring shots of the match and kicked five behinds, I said to Penny, 'You know what will happen now? We'll get the ball and score a goal.' Five goals later to Collingwood by quarter time, and the trend for the day was set. Penny bravely stuck it out until the end. She was desperately unhappy about some of the umpiring decisions but I'll venture to say that wouldn't have made a difference to the result. Tazza was on fire, Fraser looked magnificent and the rest of the boys were pretty good too!

Suffice to say, I think we'll leave that subject there. It's not a good idea to gloat when your team has defeated your partner's. After all, I've still got next year's game to face up to!

Sunday, 16 June 2002

Collingwood 12.7.79
lost to Fremantle (that's right!) 12.18.90

How the mighty are fallen! Not surprisingly, this was one I watched on TV and wished that I hadn't. It's not much consolation to remember that interstate teams have struggled all year over there — the boys looked tired and ready for their break. Hopefully Mick can weave some magic in the next two weeks.

Sunday, 30 June 2002

*Collingwood 13.15.93 defeated Kangaroos 8.12.60
(last night)*

I missed the game this week but I did make it to the breakfast! Confused? Let me explain.

It was yet another night game which means it was nigh on impossible for me to get to. In addition, I had accepted an invite to a Collingwood Players' Club breakfast today and thought the idea of a late night at the footy and then an early start for the breakfast could be a bit much. So I went to the breakfast and watched the game on television, again! After giving me kittens in the first half, the boys did the right thing and blew the game open in the third quarter to record another impressive win.

The breakfast was pretty good as well. It was for a small group and all the players were in attendance. The highlight of the morning for me was ending up with Jarrod Molloy's breakfast — or at least the one he was supposed to have. He passed it on and told the waiters to serve the guests first and I was next in line. I've got a lovely photo of it — although Hugh can't understand what the fuss is about it! Guess you had to be there!

Sunday, 7 July 2002

Collingwood 21.12.138 defeated Adelaide 17.14.116

This just goes to show that my timing is lousy and that I am never ever going to go to Football Park again. What happens? I go to the Port Adelaide game and we lose by a kick. I don't go to the Crows game and we win by four goals! Mind you, I'm not knocking the win but it should have been more! When you're nine goals up at three-quarter time, you should go ahead and record a huge percentage boosting win. Still, as Eddie said, 'We'll take a four goal win any time!'

Now, when will I call Dad? Will I do it right away or would that be too obvious? I think I'll let him sweat on it a while!

Saturday, 13 July 2002

Collingwood 15.9.99 lost to Geelong 19.13.127

Hmm, another down-to-earth thud! I didn't get to this match as I was exercising my tonsils a different way at choir practice! I did take my radio with me, though, and was not happy with what I heard. What the hell was Bucks doing smearing blood around? Not a good move and bang goes another chance at the Brownlow! Okay, put this one behind us. We've played all teams for a 10–5 win-loss ratio. I'll take that — only two more wins and we should be in the finals. I won't get too excited though. Anything can happen.

Friday, 19 July 2002

Collingwood 13.11.89 beat Richmond 7.7.49

You've guessed it, haven't you? I wasn't there again. I had every intention of going, just to prove that Collingwood could still beat Richmond with me in attendance, but then I said I'd go to a fundraiser Trivia Night and had to rely on the faithful Walkman!

Again, I had a few scary moments early on — it wasn't sounding too good up to half time. Then my favourite boy, Rupert Betheras, inspired an amazing third-quarter turn-around and in the end the boys were pretty easy winners.

I must say, there were a few Richmond supporters at the function and they were feeling pretty brave at half time. They were the same ones who had given me heaps after the crushing win in Round 1. Of course, I was grace itself when we won and only reminded them that they had lost eight in a row now and that if St Kilda beat Carlton on Sunday (and that's a coin toss) the Tigers would be second last. They were pretty quiet after that. Oh how the worm turns!

Saturday, 27 July 2002
Collingwood 8.8.56
were spanked by West Coast 17.12.114

Talk about the wheel turning! I know Subiaco's a hard place to win at, but this is downright embarrassing and, I think, their worst performance since the Carlton game in Round 3. I just hope history doesn't repeat itself against the Blues. I don't think I could face a Carlton supporter again if it did.

Friday, 2 August 2002
Collingwood 21.15.141 belted Carlton 4.9.33

Here was a match to restore faith and to make me enjoy the season again. I don't think there's a sweeter sight for a Collingwood supporter than to see 'the old enemy' i.e. Carlton, totally humiliated. Although I think the fact that this will almost certainly hand them the wooden spoon as well made it even sweeter than usual.

I had delightful company for the game as I was joined by Hugh and the aforementioned Alison. We had an enjoyable dinner and a couple of wines before the match then settled back in great anticipation — and we weren't disappointed. The match was Nathan Buckley's 200th game so the boys were obviously keen to make it a big one for the skipper and they didn't let him down (mind you he didn't let them down either).

The atmosphere was great, with the few Carlton supporters in the crowd keeping very quiet or staying for only a short time. One bad moment occurred when a somewhat officious Magpies supporter (no, that isn't a misprint) called the police over to complain about a Carlton supporter who had vented his frustration at a poor umpiring decision (yes, I'm willing to concede that) in a somewhat colourful way. We all thought it was terribly unnecessary as it wasn't as though it was ongoing bad language, so the Collingwood supporters in the crowd gave the complainant heaps once the police had sauntered off.

The last quarter was party time amongst the Collingwood supporters as we sang the club song again and again. You could almost feel sorry for the Blues — nope, not really!

Friday, 9 August 2002

Collingwood 14.13.97 lost to Hawthorn 15.15.105

We went to see *Lord of the Rings* tonight at the Astor Theatre in St Kilda. It's a very long film and the seats were very uncomfortable. We only lasted until the interval when we decided to watch the second half another time. We hadn't expected so many people to be there, obviously underestimating its popularity. As a result we ended up sitting about ten rows from the front, which isn't the best place to view such a 'big' film.

On top of that, Collingwood lost to Hawthorn. You've got to say it's one we should have won, but then Hawthorn had so much to play for — like, they're trying to get into the finals. We listened to the last quarter in the car on the way home and there was much fist pumping on my part when we hit the front in the last quarter and then even more 'turn the bloody thing off' when the Hawks got back on top and stayed there. There's a pattern forming here you know; all the 'return' games have had the opposite result to those played in the first half of the season. Oh no! On this basis we won't win again this year!

Saturday, 17 August 2002
Collingwood 10.11.71
were beaten by Essendon 19.12.126

I might be right — another reverse decision. Didn't get to the match because I was crook with a dose of bronchitis (I was even sicker by the time the final siren went). I couldn't sit through the game. I knew at quarter time that we were done and on top of everything Bucks twanged his hammy! This is a black day indeed. We're still going to make the finals but it could be really embarrassing. And how am I going to face the Bombers supporters on Monday. Now I feel even sicker!

Sunday, 25 August 2002

Collingwood 11.11.77
squeaked in over St Kilda 9.12.66

Phew! At least the first half reverse pattern has been broken and we've managed to beat one team twice. Mind you, it wasn't a pretty game and it wasn't the sort of defeat that a top four side should inflict on a cellar dweller. The game was what can only be described as an 'arm wrestle', certainly not the free-flowing game that Collingwood have been capable of. I sat there alone in the members' with my lunch and water bottle — and I can tell you my water bottle had a well-chewed look by the time the game looked safe, about two minutes before the siren went.

The good news is that with 13 wins, it looks certain that the boys will finish in the top four and have the double chance. The bad news is that if we play like we did today, I don't think a double chance will be enough!

Saturday, 31 August 2002

Collingwood 10.13.73
were defeated by Western Bulldogs 17.12.114

Bloody Terry Wallace! Why couldn't he have waited for a week to resign as Bulldogs coach? What is it about the Bulldogs coaches? They keep changing just before they play Collingwood! We've now faced up to Alan Joyce, Terry Wallace and Peter Rohde in their first games as coach of the side. The first two occasions have resulted in narrow Magpies victories. But third time lucky (for them). This time it didn't work out! It's fair to say that it wasn't a narrow loss, either. A seven-goal defeat is not the way you want to end the home and away season and face up to the finals!

I'm glad to say that I wasn't there, finally proving that they do lose when I'm not there as well as win when I am! I'm in Ballarat, celebrating my birthday.

Normally, we go away for the first week of the finals. Let's face it, there hasn't been much for me to hang around for since 1992, but this year I thought I'd be brave and keep the finals free. It doesn't do me much good because we'll be playing interstate next week. Not sure if it's Brisbane or Adelaide!

Friday, 6 September 2002 (1st Qualifying Final)
Collingwood 16.12.108
defeated Port Adelaide 14.11.95

Could someone just pinch me so I know I'm not dreaming. Collingwood defeated Port Adelaide at Football Park and are straight into the Preliminary Final!

No, I've just watched the replay (again) and I'm not dreaming. What a night it's been. I could not sit still, was punching the air, cheering, yelling at the umpire and crying — all at the same time. Hugh was pretty caught up in it too, although he did tell me to 'calm down and watch what happens' at one point! Calm down?! Impossible!

For weeks we've been hearing from the bloody South Australians that it's not fair that they might have to play a Preliminary Final at the MCG — boo hoo! Then Port finished top so looked guaranteed a home Prelim. Final. Their supporters were so confident that they saved their money for the future final and didn't turn up tonight. Of course, they're no longer guaranteed anything as they have to win next week before facing someone (probably Brisbane) away the week after! On the other hand, finals are such a novelty to Collingwood supporters that they turned up in their droves even though the match was interstate. There were about 7,000 of the Army there and they were prominent amongst a disappointing crowd of 33,000.

For me, the best thing of all (well, apart from wiping the smile off the South Australian supporters' faces and seeing Mark Williams look even more miserable) is the fact that I know I'll be able to see my boys live in the Preliminary Final at the MCG. The worry is that if Melbourne beat North and Brisbane beat Adelaide, and then Melbourne beat Adelaide in the Semi-Final — well, Collingwood could end up playing Melbourne in the Preliminary Final. And if Collingwood win, and after tonight anything's possible, then Penny will possibly never speak to me again! Is it possible I'm thinking too far ahead?

Monday, 16 September 2002

The good news is that I don't have to worry about Penny not speaking to me. Unfortunately, that's because the Crows beat the Demons on Saturday night. I really feel sorry for Penny, there's something so final about losing a final (forgive the pun). This also means that Collingwood are the only Victorian side left in the finals. Interesting that Eddie and Mick aren't calling on other club supporters to jump on — we have the Army and march alone as always!

Only five more sleeps to Saturday. Tickets are booked through the girls in the dining room, guest passes are organised. I'm going with Alison, Stuart and Tracey; this is no place for anybody but the most dedicated Magpies supporter.

Thursday, 19 September 2002

Tonight I collected my Grand Final ticket from Wayne! 'How come and who's Wayne?', I think I hear you ask. Wayne is Wayne White who, amongst other things, is my hairdresser He's also a mad Essendon supporter who keeps trying to dye my hair red and black! I've gone to the last two grand finals with Wayne and his lovely wife Becky, and we've managed to get some pretty good seats as a result of queuing or being lucky in the ballot. This year we thought we'd take the chance and the strain out of it and we booked AFL Members' packages through Elite Sports. These include prime seats, a pre-match breakfast and post-match drinks. The price was … well it wasn't cheap but I paid in April so I've forgotten now. I've been getting agitated about the tickets, especially given the Magpies' surprisingly good showing, so it's quite a relief to actually have the ticket in my hot little hands!

Only two more sleeps!

Saturday, 21 September 2002
Collingwood 13.13.91 defeated Adelaide 9.9.63

This was truly a match to savour and to hold up as an example of all that makes our great game, well — great! The weather was glorious (sunny, warm and dry), the crowd was huge (89,000 and 70,000 of them were Collingwood supporters), and the good guys won! Yay! We're into the Grand Final! Who would have believed it after that awful start to the year, after the dreadful losses to West Coast and the Doggies, after waiting eight years just to get some September action?

The day wasn't without its dramas. I did feel pretty sick when the Crows got four goals clear late in the second quarter. Then when the unknowns like Scotland and Rupert got us within a kick at half time, I could hardly breathe with nerves. I think in my heart I was sure we'd won after Pebbles kicked that ball-bursting 65-metre goal in the third quarter, but my head wouldn't say so until much, much later. In fact it went down in the record that I finally claimed victory at the 18 minute mark of the last quarter, just before Didak put it out of doubt!

I have to say that I can't remember a better day at the football — please note that I wasn't at the 1990 Grand Final! I was with three great friends, sitting among thousands of other supporters who were great friends by the end of the day. We spent the last part of the last quarter singing 'Good Old Collingwood Forever' time and again and then did the same thing on the way to the train. There was a Magpies supporter in front of me that I'd been talking to all day. As we got on top in the second half, he'd turn around with each goal to celebrate. At first we nodded, then high fives, then handshakes and by the time Nick Davis kicked the goal that took the doubt away, we were hugging like old friends. And I was crying! Yes I admit, I cried through the last ten minutes of the game.

The sight of the day was the fans leaving mid-way through the last quarter. Oh no! Not Crows supporters — but

Collingwood supporters who were rushing to get in the queue for finals tickets! I must admit to feeling a little smug as I thought about my ticket, which was sitting on the bookcase at home. No queues for me!

Sunday, 22 September 2002

I have to say the feeling is still pretty good and I'm walking around with a smile from ear to ear. Last night was fantastic! Hugh met Alison and I at the Caulfield Tabaret for drinks after the game. I knew it was a big occasion when Hugh called and suggested celebrating; he's not normally into football that much. We had a couple of bourbons and watched the end of the replay on the big screen — then I cried again. The only downer, which I hadn't realised during the game, is that Jason Cloke has been reported for striking. Having seen a replay of the incident, I think he's in trouble. It wasn't deliberate but it was clumsy and the Crow had to go off. Bugger!

On the way home we listened to the start of the Brisbane and Port game from the Gabba, and then watched it over dinner when we got in. Brisbane won, of course. The exciting thing was the Grand Final Preview where the commentators talked about Brisbane taking on Collingwood in the 'big one'. I listened and watched, and cried again!

I've come to the conclusion that my tears are as a result of years 'in the wilderness' and the strain of learning to believe that my boys can cut it on the big stage. I honestly don't think we can beat Brisbane on Saturday because I think they (Brisbane) are one of the best football teams I've ever seen, but I know that Mick and the boys think they can win and that's good enough for me.

Six more sleeps.

Monday, 23 September 2002

Work was fantastic today! Well, work was the same as normal but the atmosphere was fantastic! Everyone congratulated me as though I'd won instead of the boys. I was asked about tickets. I just smiled smugly and told them where my seat is — three rows from the fence on the 50-metre line at the City end — and that I hadn't had to queue.

I work with a lady called Kerry who is a real Brisbane supporter (she's even a member) and we've started stirring each other up. We've christened each other Lizzie Lion and Madge Magpie — not particularly brilliant, but in the spirit of the week! She queued half the night for a ticket and is sitting at the top of the Olympic stand. We reckon we're opposite each other so will send text messages through the game!

Watched the Brownlow count tonight. Thrilling television as always. Hope it's not an omen as Simon Black from Brisbane won. That means three medallists in the team. Never mind, as Jock McHale used to say, 'A champion team will always beat a team of champions.' I hope he's right.

Five more sleeps.

Tuesday, 24 September 2002

A broker asked me today if I could get him a ticket. I said no problem if he had $1000 to spend. He wasn't that keen.

As I suspected, Cloke was rubbed out for two weeks tonight. I think it was inevitable — upsetting, but inevitable. I think Collingwood will appeal, which I think is a mistake but I'm not in charge.

Four more sleeps.

Thursday, 26 September 2002

A big night tonight. Cloke's appeal was dismissed despite an impassioned speech from President Eddie. I hope there hasn't been too much focus on one player and they've planned around him not playing.

Sat back tonight, with a couple of drinks, to watch the Grand Final edition of *The Footy Show*. The show seemed so different this year, obviously because they were talking about my team and not something removed. There was a bit of a surprise in the team selection with Jarrod Molloy getting the nod for Cloke. I would have thought, with his lack of match time, that is a risk and I won't be surprised if he doesn't play. I can't believe I'm saying this, but I'd have picked Mark Richardson, especially if it rains like it's forecast.

Two more sleeps.

Friday, 27 September 2002

A really big day today! We had a Grand Final morning tea at work with pies and sausage rolls and donuts — no beer, unfortunately, but it was the thought that counted. We've also got a Grand Final sweep going where the winner has to pick winner and margin. I've gone for Collingwood by nine points. I was surprised how many people have picked the Pies. I think after the win in Adelaide there's a feeling that anything is possible, plus the weather is ordinary which might suit my boys.

I decided not to go to the parade today. It was pouring down and there were huge crowds predicted, plus I had to go to a Grand Final lunch. I've been going to these lunches for a few years now, they're an all-women affair and lots of fun. Keri came with me and we met at the venue, the Celtic Club Hotel in Queen Street, and sat back with a couple of champagnes to get us going. The guest speaker was Shane O'Sullivan who is recruiting manager at Carlton. (The question is, how much longer he will have a job given the political upheaval at the club?) We had a chance to ask questions and I tried to draw him on John Elliott but, I have to say, he's very loyal. After the talk we had a footy trivia contest which, I'm delighted to say, our team won. So we now hold the perpetual Trivia Trophy, until next year anyway.

After lunch, we headed down to the bar for a few more drinks and a bit of a flutter on the pokies. I came away a little richer, which was nice (only $5.00 but it's better than losing). We thought about staying on and listening to the band, but the smoke started to get to us both so we left for Keri's place. One nice thing happened just before we left. As we went into the bar, I had my black coat and black-and-white hat on (plus Collingwood scarf, of course) and all the people in the bar started to cheer and sing the club song. I didn't quite cry again but I was pretty chuffed, I can tell you!

Keri and I had a quiet night (I have to conserve my energy, you know). We went to see a film and then had a late supper before heading home for one last cuppa and a look at the

Grand Final Marathon — at least I watched the marathon and Keri went to bed muttering 'fanatics', I think it was.

One more sleep.

Saturday, 28 September 2002, 1.00 p.m.

Here I am in my seat waiting for history to unfold. I woke up ridiculously early this morning, thoroughly over-excited. I had early messages from Lizzie (Kerry) who is also totally over the top, as well as from fellow Magpies supporters all over Australia. I watched the North Melbourne Breakfast as I got ready and tried to stay calm and remember to breathe!

The brunch was fantastic; good food, plenty to drink, good entertainment and auction items that were way out of my league. The weather is shocking, absolutely bucketing down and I'm already soaked through. The word around the ground is there will be a late change with Molloy out and McGough or Richo in, we'll know when the teams come out I guess. Better put this away or the rain will wash the ink away. I'll be back when it's all over.

Sunday, 29 September 2002 (cont.)

I've just received an email from Penny which is so sweet:

> *What a heartbreaker! It was the best Grand Final I have seen in such a long time — the sort of match I really like, very tight. But just the sort of match you hate for your own boys to lose. They were better than gallant, they were brilliant. They just didn't get to come away with the cup and the medals. I thought*

Bucks was fabulous and, if he hadn't been awarded the Norm Smith medal, I reckon Rocca should have got it. I'll try to catch up for a wake this week, either tomorrow or Wednesday, okay? Be brave little Buckaroo.

And you know what? She's right …

they were brilliant, they did nothing wrong, they just didn't win.

And I'm so proud of them. What's more, they've given me and thousands like me reason to believe again. So, watch out all of you next year, we'll be back and this time — well, we'll see what happens!

Defeated not vanquished; Dawn and Mick at the Copeland Trophy Night 2002.

Afterword

The stories in this book are *not* fictitious. No bull — maybe some poetic licence but absolutely, definitely, and emphatically no bull! Nor are the characters portrayed in this book fictitious. We, Dawn and Penny, are real women. There is no mystery about us. What you see is pretty much what you get. And, as you've probably guessed by now, we love our footy — in fact, we are positively passionate about it.

The title of our book, *Real Women Love Footy*, is not intended as a criticism; we do not hold that only women who are passionate about their footy are 'real' women. Rather the title is meant to be an affirmative statement that women can and do *really* love football; and that those who do are as *real* as any other women.

Eddie McGuire says:

> *It's embarrassing and demeaning to suggest to women they watch football because of the sexy shorts. That might be good for 10 seconds, but they stay for the whole game.*[11]

Women who love their football like we do are not ... well, not necessarily, anyway ... wacky, lacking in intelligence, juvenile, macho, voyeuristic, ridiculous, or even from another planet. We are proud to discuss our shared passion and equally enjoy encouraging others to partake of it — the more the merrier, we say ... and we've been known to get *very* merry!

Football *is* a legitimate subject for women's interest and passion. Women are passionate about it, and particularly about the Australian Football League. We are clearly not alone. 'Statistics show that women now represent 46% of all AFL crowds'[12] and 51% of the membership of the sixteen AFL clubs.[13] Football is no longer, if indeed it ever has been, an exclusively male domain. Whilst the game is played by men exclusively at the elite level, it is supported by women and men alike — *real* people.

> *The bottom line is that, with so many women enjoying their own disposable income nowadays, women members equal big business — and the clubs know it. They also know that women make fiercely loyal fans, through bad times and good.*[14]

We have endeavoured, in this book, to celebrate football from the female point of view, rather than celebrate women as devoted football fans or preach to the converted (i.e. other female football fans) about how best to go about enjoying their football. We will have achieved our aim if the reader has gained some appreciation of the realities of supporting one's football team as a female football devotee.

We are unabashed in our enthusiasm and
exuberance for football.

We do not apologise for being out there and 'in your face' with our excitement and views about the game in general, and about our respective clubs in particular. Haven't we come a long way from the 'closet' footy fans, afraid to overtly express our interest in football for fear of ridicule, that we were all those years ago?

Endnotes

1 Figures provided by Tim Gaspar (Business Development Manager, Commercial), Melbourne Football Club, November 2001.

2 Melbourne Football Club Record Issue 2001, p. 20.

3 Figures provided by Tim Gaspar, (Business Development Manager, Commercial), Melbourne Football Club, November 2001.

4 Figures provided by Dean Frost (Marketing Operations Manager), Melbourne Football Club, May 1999.

5 ibid.

6 'Bruce' is a French word meaning 'brushwood thicket; woods' according to a book called *35,000+ Baby Names* by Bruce (and he ought to know) Lansky, Lothian Books, 1996, p. 273.

7 For those who don't watch the show or who are from another planet, on the episode of *The Footy Show* that followed Melbourne's 80+ point loss to Collingwood in 2001, Sam Newman (in a pre-arranged gag) pushed a cream pie into the face of David Schwarz. Schwarz pushed Newman to the ground and an ugly incident was only averted by Eddie McGuire's intervention. A huge outcry occurred with even Schwarz's mother, Mary, getting involved. As a result, Schwarz went back onto the show the following week and admitted he had agreed with Newman that 'something' would be done in a bid to prod his team-mates to a better performance.

8 Sheahan, M 2003 'Cyclone David's Early Warning', *Herald Sun*, 18 June, p. 85

9   J Ross, *The Clubs: The Complete History of Every Club in the VFL/AFL*, Penguin Books Australia Ltd, 1998, p. 256.

10   ibid., p. 255.

11   J Wiles, M Fincke, & C George, 'Why women love footy', *The Australian Women's Weekly*, September 1999, p. 67.

12   Tim Gaspar (MFC Business Development Manager), Melbourne Football Club Membership Magazine 2002, p. 5

13   Figures provided by Dean Frost (Marketing Operations Manager), Melbourne Football Club, May 1999.

14   Wiles et al., p. 68.